STEP-BY-STEP

Good for Your Heart Cookbook

STEP-BY-STEP

Good for Your Heart Cookbook

Consultant Editor
Helen Middleton

LORENZ BOOKS
LONDON • NEW YORK • SYDNEY • BATH

This edition published in 1997 by Lorenz Books

Lorenz Books is an imprint of
Anness Publishing Limited
Hermes House
88-89 Blackfriars Road
London SE1 8HA

© 1997 Anness Publishing Limited

ISBN 1 85967 366 X

A CIP catalogue record for this book is available from the British Library

Publisher: Joanna Lorenz
Senior Cookery Editor: Linda Fraser
Project Editor: Rosemary Wilkinson
Jacket Designer: Brian Weldon
Designers: Peter Laws, Lilian Lindblom, Alan Marshall and Brian Weldon
Photographers: James Duncan, Michelle Garrett, Amanda Heywood, David Jordan,
Don Last and Peter Reilly
Stylists: Madeleine Brehaut, Jo Harris, Fiona Tillett and Judy Williams
Recipes: Catherine Atkinson, Christine France, Carole Handslip, Sue Maggs, Annie
Nichols, Anne Sheasby and Liz Trigg

For all recipes, quantities are given in both metric and imperial
measures, and, where appropriate, measures are also given in standard
cups and spoons. Follow one set, but not a mixture, because they are
not interchangeable.

Note: Nutritional information is provided per portion for all recipes. Where a
recipe serves, for example, 4–6, the information is based on the smaller portion.

Printed and bound in Hong Kong

1 3 5 7 9 10 8 6 4 2

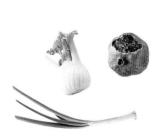

CONTENTS

INTRODUCTION

Making changes to our diet and to our lifestyle can help us reduce the risk of coronary heart disease (CHD). There are three main things we can do to improve our way of life:
we can become more active – take 30 minutes moderate exercise five times a week; we can give up smoking – see a doctor or call one of the helplines for advice; and we can learn to cope with stress.

If we also improve our diet, we will enhance these changes and in addition will help to control the other major risk factors of CHD, which are: raised blood cholesterol, raised blood pressure and obesity (or being overweight).

Eating for a healthy heart isn't difficult. As a first step, eat at least five portions of vegetables and/or fruit a day, and make sure that at least half your meals consist of starchy foods like bread, pasta, rice and potatoes, without too much added fat. Even simple changes to eating habits can make a considerable difference. Cooking our own food puts us in control and makes it easy to limit the amount of fat (particularly saturated fat), salt and sugar we consume. The recipes in this collection prove just how delicious a well-balanced diet can be, and there are numerous techniques and suggestions for eliminating the less desirable elements in our food while retaining – and even enhancing – the flavour.

So, change to a healthier lifestyle and follow the food recommendations in this book, then relax and enjoy life – it'll do your heart good.

Eating Less Salt

One of the steps we can take to reduce our risk of coronary heart disease is to cut down on the amount of salt we eat. Excessive salt intake can be linked to high blood pressure and is one of the main reasons why blood pressure tends to rise as we get older. (Other risk factors include low potassium intake and being overweight.)

Salt, together with potassium, is essential for a variety of bodily functions, but we tend to have far too much of it, largely through our consumption of processed foods. Canned, pre-packaged or "convenience" foods, takeaways and ready-prepared meals, contribute as much as 80 per cent of the salt in our diet, so preparing and cooking more of our own food is an excellent way of reducing our daily intake to the recommended 6g.

Eating more non-processed foods – such as fresh vegetables, fruit, fish and meat – will have an added bonus in boosting our potassium levels.

Although cutting down on the amount of salt used during cooking and at the table is not enough on its own, it is a valuable step in helping to re-educate our tastebuds. The more salt we have, the more we want. Gradually reduce the amount added and what used to taste delicious soon seems excessively salty.

It's also a good idea to note which foods are high in salt and keep a check on how many of these we eat.

CUTTING DOWN
We often add salt out of habit, the following are some tips to help you cut down.

- Taste food before you shake on salt – and then use it only sparingly.
- Block up some of the holes in the salt cellar.
- Better still, do not add any kind of salt, including most salt substitutes to your food, either when cooking or to the finished dish at the table.
- Replace salt in recipes with herbs and spices, garlic and lemon juice, mustard or chilli powder. A small quantity of wine or beer can also be added for extra flavour.
- Use fresh or frozen vegetables instead of canned.
- Chinese food in particular tends to be high in monosodium glutamate and salt, so enjoy it as an occasional treat, or make your own.
- Cook with a stock made from celery, onion, carrot and bouquet garni instead of stock cubes.
- Swap to lower salt breads. Most breads contain

2 per cent salt, but read the labels. "Healthy eating" brands of bread can contain as little as 0.8 per cent salt and some health food stores sell bread baked with no added salt at all.

Above: *There's a marvellous variety of fresh fruit now available all year round.*

include cured and smoked meat; smoked fish; canned meats; cottage cheese; salted butter and margarine/low-fat spreads; savoury crackers, salted crisps, salted nuts and similar savoury snacks; some sweet biscuits; baked beans and canned vegetables; fish canned in brine; olives; sauces (ketchup, brown sauce, soy sauce, Worcester-shire sauce); and stock cubes (unless salt-free).

Some foods, although relatively high in salt, provide other important nutrients, and so should be enjoyed in moderation, unless your doctor suggests otherwise. These include hard cheeses, canned oily fish and break-fast cereals (choose varieties with little or no salt).

FOOD WITH MODERATE TO LOW SALT CONTENT

These include fresh fruit and vegetables; wholemeal flour and pasta; brown rice; breakfast cereals without added salt (puffed wheat, shredded wheat, porridge oats); unsalted butter and low-salt spreads; unsalted nuts; dried fruit; pulses; oatmeal and oats; milk; fresh fish; poultry; game; meat; and eggs.

Right: *Fresh vegetables can be used in a wide range of soups, side dishes and main courses.*

LOW-SALT VEGETABLE STOCK

This is a good way of making use of left-over vegetables and will produce a healthy, full-flavoured stock.

INGREDIENTS
1 onion
2 carrots
2 large celery sticks, plus any
    small amounts from the
    following: leeks, celeriac,
    parsnip, turnip, cabbage or
    cauliflower trimmings,
    mushroom peelings
30ml/2 tbsp vegetable oil
bouquet garni
6 black peppercorns

1 Peel, halve and slice the onion. Roughly chop the remaining vegetables.

2 Heat the oil in a large pan and fry the onion and vegetables until soft and lightly browned. Add the remaining ingredients and cover with 1.7 litres/ 3 pints/7 cups water.

3 Bring to the boil, skim the surface then partially cover and simmer for 1½ hours. Strain the stock and allow to cool. Store in a covered container in the refrigerator for 2–3 days.

Eating Less Fat

Another essential factor in the healthy diet is to reduce the amount of fat we eat, particularly the amount of saturated fat. This lowers our blood cholesterol levels, which, in turn, reduces the risk of CHD. At the moment 15–16 per cent of the calories we eat are from saturated fat. It is recommended that this is reduced to no more than 10 per cent.

WHERE DO SATURATED FATS COME FROM?

As a general rule, saturated fats are solid at room temperature. The list includes lard, butter, hard cheese and the visible fat on meat. Saturated fats can also be "hidden" in products such as pork pies, cakes, biscuits, ice cream, pastry and chocolate. The major sources of saturated fats are full-fat dairy products (milk, cheese, cream), followed by fatty meat products (pies, pasties, sausages).

HOW MUCH FAT?

It is not a good idea to eliminate fat from our diet entirely. Limited amounts of some fats are essential for good health. The ideal is no more than three portions of fat per day. A portion equals:
• 5ml/1 tsp butter, margarine or cooking oil;
• 10ml/2 tsp low-fat spread;
• 5ml/1 tsp salad dressing or mayonnaise.

It is preferable to choose polyunsaturated fats, such as those found in vegetable oils, spreads or margarines labelled as being high in polyunsaturates, and oily fish.

Meat is a valuable source of protein, iron, B vitamins and minerals, while dairy foods contribute calcium, protein, B vitamins and vitamins A and D. To continue to benefit from these important nutrients, choose lean meat and low-fat dairy products where possible and eat in moderation.

Most of us will come to no harm if we eat the occasional high-fat food, but as a general rule, it is wise to be wary of cream, cream-based desserts, chocolate, crisps, Danish pastries, cakes, ice cream, rich sauces and gravies, confectionery, fatty bacon, sausages and other meat products.

LOW-FAT SWAPS

Make low-fat substitutes wherever possible, such as:
• skimmed or semi-skimmed milk for full fat milk;
• low-fat yogurt for full-fat varieties;
• small amounts of lean meat for fatty meat products, e.g. sausages, sausage rolls, pâtés, luncheon meats, meat pies and pasties;
• swap two meat meals a week with fish, especially oily fish (such as sardines, pilchards, herring, mackerel and salmon), which provide "omega 3" fatty acids. These fatty acids help to reduce blood viscosity, making it less likely to clot.

Right: *Eat a variety of white and oily fish, such as tuna, plaice, salmon, trout and mackerel.*

High Fibre Foods

People who eat a diet rich in fibre tend to have lower blood cholesterol levels and are at a lower risk of CHD than those whose diet consists largely of refined foods. High fibre foods are also filling, which can be an asset when it comes to weight control. There are many types of fibre, but one in particular, soluble fibre, seems to be beneficial in binding cholesterol and preventing it from being deposited in the arteries.

SOURCES OF FIBRE

Foods high in soluble fibre include oats; beans and peas; apples and oranges; and green leafy vegetables, such as cabbage and spinach. To be effective sources of fibre, these vegetables need to be cooked and eaten without additional fats, so do not fry them or smother vegetables with butter or fatty sauces.

The best high fibre foods are those in which the fibre occurs naturally, such as cereals, vegetables and fruit. These foods are also rich in the protective antioxidant vitamin beta carotene, vitamins C and E and the minerals zinc, selenium, manganese and copper. Antioxidants are substances that delay or prevent oxidation, which is the process by which oxygen combines with other substances. A by-product of oxidation is the production of free radicals. Free radicals in a living organism can be extremely harmful. One of their effects is to damage artery walls, allowing cholesterol to be deposited and thus increasing the risk of heart disease. We cannot avoid encountering free radicals because we breathe oxygen and pollutants, such as cigarette smoke and chemicals, but we can limit their effect.

EATING MORE FIBRE

The easiest way to boost your fibre intake is to:
- Eat plenty of bread, pasta, rice and potatoes. Choose wholemeal bread and pasta, brown rice and eat skins on potatoes.
- Instead of buying biscuits and cakes, which can be high in sugar, salt and fats, bake wholemeal scones, muffins or fruited buns. Serve them plain or with a mere scraping of low-fat spread.
- Enjoy plenty of breakfast cereal (with low-fat milk and no sugar) but choose whole-grain varieties with little or no added sugar e.g. shredded wheat, puffed wheat, porridge oats and muesli. Avoid sugar-coated cereals.
- Use more pulses (beans, peas, lentils, split peas) either alone or to replace some of the meat in dishes like cottage pie, shepherd's pie, curry, pasta sauces or chilli con carne. Make frequent use of canned beans, including baked beans.
- Eat at least five portions of vegetables and/or fruit every day.

AVOID BRAN

Bran added to refined food is not as good for you as starchy foods, vegetables and fruits. Too much raw bran can bind minerals, making them unavailable to the body. Bran may conquer constipation, but it does not share the cholesterol-lowering effect of other fibres that are found in starchy foods, fresh vegetables and fruits.

Right: *Bread, pasta, potatoes, rice and muesli are all good sources of fibre.*

Cholesterol

Cholesterol is a waxy substance that occurs naturally in the body, when it is referred to as blood cholesterol. It is also present in foods of animal origin (dietary cholesterol). The higher the level of cholesterol in the blood, the greater our risk of heart disease. Some cholesterol is essential for functions such as the making of cell membranes, and the body usually maintains a balance, making more if needed. However, if the blood contains too much cholesterol, this can cause problems.

GOOD AND BAD CHOLESTEROL

There are two main types of blood cholesterol. The "good" type is high density lipoprotein (HDL), which carries excess cholesterol to the liver for removal from the body. The "bad" type is low density lipoprotein (LDL), which deposits cholesterol on the artery walls. Adequate amounts of HDL lower the risk of coronary heart disease, but excessive amounts of LDL raise the risk.

At one time, it was thought that cholesterol-rich foods were largely responsible for high blood cholesterol levels, but it is now known that the amount of cholesterol we eat is not as significant as our intake of fats. Saturated fats are, once again, the villains of the piece, leading to increased levels of LDL.

WHERE IS CHOLESTEROL FOUND?

Although the link between dietary cholesterol and blood cholesterol is disputed, it can be useful to know which foods are cholesterol-rich. Dietary cholesterol is found only in animal foods: the richest sources are liver, shellfish and eggs. The general advice is to eat no more than four eggs a week. If you like mussels, crabs, prawns, shrimps and other shellfish (which although high in cholesterol, are low in fat), eat them in moderation. Grill, barbecue or cook shellfish in paella and risotto. Serve them, oriental-style in thin broth, but not in creamy French seafood dishes.

High levels of cholesterol are also found in fatty meat, high-fat cheeses and full-fat milk, but as we have seen, eating for a healthy heart limits these foods anyway. They do not have to be given up completely, just eaten in sensible proportions.

READ THE LABELS

Nutritional labels state how much fat a food contains. Some even state what percentage is saturated but very few labels give information on cholesterol. If there is no statistical data on the label, ingredients are listed in descending order by weight. Common names for saturated fat on food labels include hydrogenated vegetable oil or fat; palm oil; coconut oil; cocoa butter; shortening (solid vegetable fat); animal fat; milk solids and non-milk fat. If any of these names appears high up the list of ingredients, the food is likely to be high in saturated fat.

Above: *Make plenty of salad and cooked vegetable dishes and avoid adding too much fat to your diet.*

Life is for Living

People who exercise regularly have lower levels of coronary heart disease, and those with CHD who exercise are less likely to die as a result of the disease. Most people need to take more exercise but how much is enough? Taking positive action to stop smoking and to lower your stress levels is also an excellent way of getting a healthier lifestyle, while alcohol needs to be treated with caution.

HOW MUCH PHYSICAL ACTIVITY SHOULD YOU DO?

Until recently 20 minutes of vigorous aerobic exercise three times a week was the prescription for preventing CHD. New research, however, shows that even moderate amounts of less intense exercise can be beneficial.

Because we are all so sedentary, even getting out of the chair and taking some exercise for half an hour, once or twice a week can have a positive effect. Regular exercise – 30 minutes of moderate intensity for five days out of seven – has substantial benefits.

Exercise of moderate intensity makes you breathe slightly harder. Your heart rate will be slightly raised, so you will feel warmer, but will not be out of breath.

MODERATE INTENSITY ACTIVITY

Aerobic capacity varies between individuals, but examples of moderate intensity activity include: brisk walking (5–6 kph/ 4 mph); heavy do-it-yourself work in the home; gardening (such as raking leaves or using a power mower); washing the car; doing strenuous housework and lifting or carrying heavy loads. Golf, table tennis, social dancing and keep-fit (all at an intensity that makes you breathe hard and sweat a little) are also worthwhile, as are slow stair climbing, cycling at more than 16 kph/ 10 mph, gentle swimming, playing doubles tennis and doing low-intensity aerobic exercises.

SMOKING

Many doctors consider smoking to be the biggest risk factor when it comes to CHD, with the risk increasing relative to the number of years someone has smoked and how many cigarettes have been smoked.

The harmful effects are linked to carbon monoxide in the smoke (which decreases the amount of oxygen to the heart) and nicotine (which makes the heart work harder). In a person with CHD this may lead to disturbances in heart rhythm. Both nicotine and carbon monoxide increase the tendency for blood to clot. Free radicals in smoke also increase damage to the artery walls, making it easier for cholesterol to be deposited.

STRESS

Despite the popular view that top grade executives with high levels of responsibility are most likely to suffer stress, current research suggests that it is often the lower grade workers whose jobs make high demands but who have low control over their work (and lives) who suffer more CHD. Research continues into stress and heart disease. Meanwhile it seems that good relaxation techniques, job satisfaction and leisure-time physical activity help us to cope with stress and probably reduce the risk of CHD.

ALCOHOL

Light and moderate drinkers appear to have a lower death rate from CHD than either non-drinkers or heavy drinkers. Light to moderate means 1–3 units a day, or not more than 21 per week for women/28 for men; possibly up to 28 a week for post-menopausal women. Protection may be the result of alcohol raising levels of HDL cholesterol in the blood. Another factor may be the antioxidant properties of some drinks, mainly red wine. If you are a light to moderate drinker, the advice seems to be that it is reasonable to continue, provided that you have your doctor's blessing, but the other risks associated with alcohol outweigh any advice to start drinking or to increase the amount of alcohol you drink. Remember, however, that alcohol is very fattening.

Meal Planning

If all your meals contain generous portions of fresh vegetables, fruit and starchy foods, together with small portions of dairy food or meat, fish and vegetarian alternatives, you cannot go too far wrong.

Eating for a healthy heart does not mean certain foods are entirely forbidden, but it does mean:
• cutting down on foods that contain a lot of fat, and saturated fat in particular, such as dairy products, meat products, cakes, biscuits, fatty snacks and confectionery, especially chocolate;
• switching to low-fat dairy produce, cooking with lean meat rather than eating meat pies or pasties, and eating plenty of fish, lean poultry, beans and pulses;
• using limited amounts of low-fat spreads and oils.

Above: *Broccoli and almond soup - a good recipe for lunchtime.*

SAMPLE MENUS

Breakfast
Choose one of the following:
• wholemeal toast with a thin scraping of low-fat spread and preserve
• whole-grain cereal with skimmed milk (add fresh or dried fruit)
• fruit (fresh or dried fruit compote) and low-fat natural yogurt
• poached egg or fish, or boiled egg with wholemeal toast
• wholemeal bun or muffin
• porridge with skimmed milk.

Lunch
Try one of the following ideas:
• wholemeal sandwiches or rolls with a small amount of lean meat, fish or cheese and lots of salad
• vegetable-based soup with a wholemeal roll
• wholemeal quiche with a baked potato and salad
• rice or pasta salad
• a baked potato with a large mixed salad and a small amount of lean meat or cheese
• baked beans on toast.

Above: *Leek and caraway gratin makes a full-flavoured main meal.*

Above: *Fresh citrus jelly – a light and refreshing pudding.*

Above: *A chicken sandwich makes a tasty and nutritious snack.*

MAIN MEAL

Try one of these suggestions:

- hearty soup, such as minestrone
- wholemeal pasta or risotto with vegetable-based sauce
- grilled fish or meat plus vegetables and/or salad
- a baked potato with chilli con carne (or vegetarian equivalent)
- a stir-fry made with a small amount of lean meat or fish with plenty of vegetables and using polyunsaturated oil, served with rice
- vegetable and pulse or pasta casserole with wholemeal cobbler or potato topping.

PUDDINGS

Strictly speaking, puddings are not necessary, but as we enjoy them, let's use them to add more fruit and low-fat dairy produce to the diet. The following provide essential nutrients without excessive amounts of fat:

Fresh fruit; fruit salad with yogurt or low-fat frozen yogurt (occasionally with ice cream); canned fruit salad in fruit juice; dried fruit compote; bread and butter pudding or rice pudding (made with low-fat milk and added fruit); wholemeal pancakes filled with fruit purée; home-made fruit crumble; strudel with low-fat filo pastry; real fruit jelly; fresh fruit fool made with reduced-fat cream or yogurt or low-fat custard; fruit brûlée made with thick yogurt instead of cream; sorbet; fruit kebab; fruit tart.

SNACKS

If you are watching your weight, snacks are not a good idea, but they are often necessary for children, teenagers, pregnant women and very active people. Next time you feel the need for a snack, choose something from the list that follows. It will do you much more good than a chocolate bar or a packet of crisps:

Fresh fruit; 1–2 slices of bread (all varieties); a wholemeal sandwich or a couple of slices of toast; a small slice of fruit cake or malt loaf; a spiced fruited bun or fruit scone (plain or with a scraping of low-fat spread); a bowl of breakfast cereal; 2–3 plain biscuits; a few unsalted nuts or seeds; a tub of yogurt or a yogurt drink; a semi-skimmed milk shake; plain popcorn or a few unsalted pretzels.

Healthy Cooking Techniques

The aims of cooking for a healthy heart are to avoid adding fat to food, to reduce the saturated fat content of the ingredients where possible, to use techniques that retain the vitamins and minerals and, of course, to ensure that the food is delicious by preserving or enhancing its flavour, colour and texture.

STIR-FRYING

This method means that food cooks quickly to retain maximum nutritional value, colour and texture.

Slivers of meat can be marinated in savoury mixtures of, for example, soy sauce, fruit juice, tomato purée and vinegar, or similar sauces before cooking to tenderize them and add flavour.

Foods need to be cut into small pieces, so that they cook quickly and evenly.

2 Add garlic to flavour a stir-fry for a few seconds, then add the meat.

1 Preheat the wok, then dribble only 5–10ml/1–2 tsp oil around the rim. Cut meat into thin slivers or cubes to minimize cooking time.

3 Once the meat is almost cooked add the other ingredients.

STEAMING

Food is cooked over boiling liquid (usually water) but it does not touch the liquid. As a result most of the vitamins and minerals are retained.

Browning is not part of the process, so fat need never be added.

Steaming preserves the texture of foods and is a good cooking method for those who prefer their vegetables with a bit of bite. It is also very useful for fish, poultry and puddings.

1 Prepare ingredients as for stir-frying. Expandable steamers will fit a range of saucepan sizes. Add food straight into the steamer and cover.

2 If using a bamboo steamer over either a wok or pan of boiling liquid, place the food in a bowl first, then cover.

MICROWAVING

This is a quick and useful way of cooking vegetables, fruit and fish.

Naturally moist foods are cooked without additional liquid, and only a small amount of liquid is added to other foods. As a result, vitamins and minerals do not leach out into cooking water which is then thrown away.

Fat is not required for cooking, and microwaved food can be seasoned with fresh chopped herbs instead of salt. The flavour can be sharpened by adding a little lemon juice.

Place food in a microwave-proof dish, or wrap in a paper parcel. Refer to the manufacturer's handbook for information on power levels and cooking times.

CASSEROLING

One-pot meals are good for stress-free entertaining. They also have the advantage that vitamins and minerals are retained in the stock, which is served alongside the other ingredients.

Use only the minimum amount of fat for cooking and make the casserole a day ahead, then cool and chill it. Any fat will solidify on the surface and can easily be lifted off before the casserole is re-heated.

Trim visible fat from meat or remove skin from poultry.

PRESSURE COOKING

This method cuts cooking time dramatically, which encourages the frequent consumption of beneficial low-fat foods (brown rice cooks in 7 minutes, potatoes in 6). Like steaming, pressure cooking retains more nutrients because the food is not in contact with the cooking water.

GRILLING

There's no need to add fat when grilling meat, fish or vegetables. Use a rack and any fat that runs from the meat can easily be drained. Brush the rack with oil before cooking to prevent the food from sticking. Cook under a preheated grill and baste with lemon juice, if necessary.

POACHING

This is an excellent way of cooking delicate white fish (plaice) or whole oily fish (mackerel, salmon, trout). Fish steaks, particularly cod, halibut, salmon and tuna also cook well by either method and there is no need to add any fat.

Poaching can be done either in the oven or on top of the cooker.

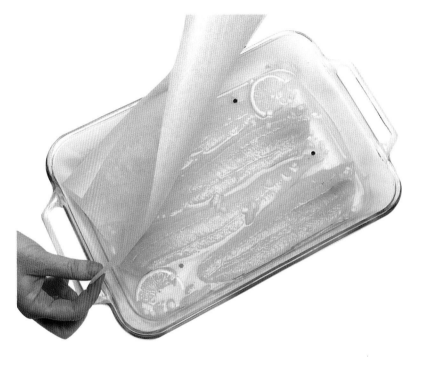

To oven-poach fish, pour in boiling liquid to barely cover the fish, add any flavourings and cover with buttered greaseproof paper. Cook in a pre-heated oven to 180°C/350°F/Gas 4.

To poach on top of the cooker, suspend the fish in the poaching liquid, either in a muslin hammock or on a rack. Cover with liquid, bring to the boil and simmer gently until cooked.

Equipment

There are various pieces of equipment which will help you to prepare food with a minimum amount of fat. Some do not need you to add any fat at all, others allow the fat to drain away.

bamboo steamer

wok with draining wire and lid

STEAMERS

These may be oval or round and consist of two pans, a lower one, which holds the boiling water or stock and a perforated upper pan, which holds the food. Steam enters via the holes, and is trapped by a lid on the top pan. Metal steaming baskets that stand inside a saucepan are suitable for steaming small quantities of food. A metal colander sitting inside a saucepan can also be used as a steamer; find a saucepan lid which will fit on top, or make a lid to cover from foil.

Bamboo steamers come in a range of sizes with multiple layers and will fit either over a saucepan or inside a wok.

ROASTING GADGETS

Placing meat on a trivet or a rack in a roasting tin will allow the fat to drain from the meat. Do not add fat. Cover the meat with foil if necessary to prevent it from drying out. Chicken roasters hold the chicken so that it stands upright in the roasting tin. This is an efficient way of draining the fat.

PASTRY BRUSHES

These inexpensive items are useful for brushing pans and baking tins with a minimal amount of oil.

WOK

This is the perfect utensil for stir-frying. Thanks to its spherical shape, the heat spreads from the base upwards so all the ingredients receive an equal amount of heat.

A new wok should be seasoned before it is used for the first time. Wash and dry the wok thoroughly. Heat the dry wok, then remove it from the heat and rub a little oil and salt on to the surface. Return the wok to a high heat for a few seconds, until the oil burns off. Allow to cool, wipe and use. It should not be necessary to wash the wok again – just wipe it clean after use with kitchen paper.

BARBECUE GRILL BASKETS

These allow food to be held securely when placed over the hot coals, at the same time importantly allowing fat to drain away. Non-stick versions are available.

NON-STICK PANS
Good quality non-stick frying pans, saucepans and grill pans allow food to be cooked by any method, even frying, without additional fat. Food can also be sweated or sautéed with the minimal amount of added fat.

Pans with ribbed bases allow any fat that drains from meat to be poured away.

Heavy-based cast iron pans of good quality also allow cooking on the hob without added fat.

GRAVY SEPARATOR
Available as a glass or plastic jug or ceramic "boat", this item has a low-set spout that takes gravy from the bottom of the jug and avoids the fat floating on the surface of the gravy when being poured.

MOULI OR BLENDER
Use one of these handy appliances to purée vegetables in order to thicken sauces instead of adding a roux, cornflour or eggs.

BULB BASTER
This works like a syringe when the bulb at the top is squeezed, sucking up fat from the roasting tin.

Although conventionally used as a means of basting a roast with fat, in the hands of a health-conscious cook the utensil proves ideal for skimming fat from soups, sauces and casseroles.

Above: *Choose pans with heavy bottoms, sturdy insulated handles and tight-fitting lids.*

Melon and Basil Soup

A deliciously refreshing, chilled fruit soup, just right for a hot summer's day.

Serves 4–6

INGREDIENTS
2 Charentais or rock melons
75 g/3 oz/⅓ cup caster sugar
175 ml/6 fl oz/¾ cup water
finely grated rind and juice of 1 lime
45 ml/3 tbsp shredded fresh basil
fresh basil leaves, to garnish

basil

caster sugar

lime

Charentais melon

NUTRITIONAL NOTES
PER PORTION:

ENERGY 63Kcals/268KJ PROTEIN 0.28g
FAT 0.09g SATURATED FAT 0g
CARBOHYDRATE 16g
FIBRE 0.25g SUGAR 16.2g
SODIUM 17.3mg

1 Cut the melons in half across the middle. Scrape out the seeds and discard. Using a melon baller, scoop out 20–24 balls and set aside for the garnish. Scoop out the remaining flesh and place in a blender or food processor.

2 Place the sugar, water and lime zest in a small pan over a low heat. Stir until dissolved, bring to the boil and simmer for 2–3 minutes. Remove from the heat and leave to cool slightly. Pour half the mixture into the blender or food processor with the melon flesh. Blend until smooth, adding the remaining syrup and lime juice to taste.

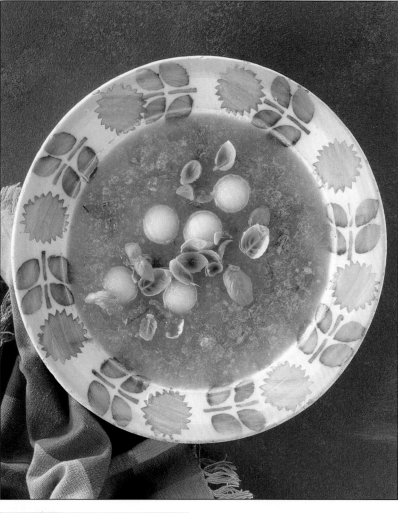

3 Pour the mixture into a bowl, stir in the basil and chill. Serve garnished with basil leaves and melon balls.

COOK'S TIP
Add the syrup in two stages, as the amount of sugar needed will depend on the sweetness of the melon.

Leek, Parsnip and Ginger Soup

A flavoursome winter warmer, with the added spiciness of fresh ginger.

Serves 4–6

INGREDIENTS
30 ml/2 tbsp olive oil
225 g/8 oz leeks, sliced
25 g/1 oz fresh ginger root, finely
   chopped
675 g/1½ lb parsnips, roughly
   chopped
300 ml/½ pint/1¼ cups dry white
   wine
1.1 litres/2 pints/5 cups vegetable
   stock or water
salt and freshly ground black pepper
low-fat fromage blanc, to garnish
paprika, to garnish

ginger

parsnips

vegetable stock

leek

1 Heat the oil in a large pan and add the leeks and ginger. Cook gently for 2–3 minutes, until the leeks start to soften.

2 Add the parsnips and cook for a further 7–8 minutes.

NUTRITIONAL NOTES
PER PORTION:

ENERGY 165Kcals/692KJ PROTEIN 3.4g
FAT 6.5g SATURATED FAT 0.99g
CARBOHYDRATE 16.4g
FIBRE 6g SUGAR 8.2g
SODIUM 17mg

3 Pour in the wine and stock or water and bring to the boil. Reduce the heat and simmer for 20–30 minutes or until the parsnips are tender.

4 Purée in a blender until smooth. Season to taste. Reheat and garnish with a swirl of fromage blanc and a light dusting of paprika.

Broccoli and Almond Soup

The creaminess of the toasted almonds combines perfectly with the slight bitterness of the taste of broccoli.

Serves 4–6

INGREDIENTS
50 g/2 oz/⅔ cup ground almonds
675 g/1½ lb broccoli
850 ml/1½ pints/3¾ cups vegetable
    stock or water
300 ml/½ pint/1¼ cups skimmed
    milk
salt and freshly ground black pepper

ground almonds

skimmed milk

broccoli

1 Preheat the oven to 180°C/350°F/Gas 4. Spread the ground almonds evenly on a baking sheet and toast in the oven for about 10 minutes, or until golden. Reserve ¼ of the almonds and set aside for the garnish.

2 Cut the broccoli into small florets and steam for 6–7 minutes or until tender.

3 Place the remaining toasted almonds, broccoli, stock or water and milk in a blender and blend until smooth. Season to taste.

4 Reheat the soup and serve sprinkled with the reserved toasted almonds.

Chilled Fresh Tomato Soup

This effortless uncooked soup can be made in minutes.

Serves 4–6

INGREDIENTS

1.5 kg/3–3½ lb ripe tomatoes, peeled
   and roughly chopped
4 garlic cloves, crushed
30 ml/2 tbsp balsamic vinegar
freshly ground black pepper
4 slices wholemeal bread
low-fat fromage blanc, to garnish

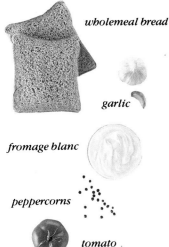

wholemeal bread

garlic

fromage blanc

peppercorns

tomato

COOK'S TIP

For the best flavour, it is important to use only fully ripened, flavourful tomatoes in this soup.

1 Place the tomatoes in a blender with the garlic and olive oil if using. Blend until smooth.

2 Pass the mixture through a sieve to remove the seeds. Stir in the balsamic vinegar and season to taste with pepper. Leave in the fridge to chill.

NUTRITIONAL NOTES

PER PORTION:

ENERGY 104Kcals/436KJ PROTEIN 5.42g
FAT 1.4g SATURATED FAT 0.1g
CARBOHYDRATE 19.22g
FIBRE 3.9g SUGAR 3.97g
SODIUM 160.33mg

3 Toast the bread lightly on both sides. Whilst still hot, cut off the crusts and slice in half horizontally. Place the toast on a board with the uncooked sides facing down and, using a circular motion, rub to remove any doughy pieces of bread.

4 Cut each slice into 4 triangles. Place on a grill pan and toast the uncooked sides until lightly golden. Garnish each bowl of soup with a spoonful of fromage blanc and serve with the melba toast.

Broccoli and Chestnut Terrine

Served hot or cold, this versatile terrine is equally suitable for a dinner party as for a picnic.

Serves 4–6

NUTRITIONAL NOTES
PER PORTION:
ENERGY 164Kcals/691KJ PROTEIN 9.84g
FAT 5.8g SATURATED FAT 2.08g
CARBOHYDRATE 19.29g
FIBRE 3.97g SUGAR 4.65g
SODIUM 147mg

INGREDIENTS
450 g/1 lb broccoli, cut into small florets
225 g/8 oz cooked chestnuts, roughly chopped
50 g/2 oz/1 cup fresh wholemeal breadcrumbs
60 ml/4 tbsp low-fat natural yogurt
30 ml/2 tbsp Parmesan cheese, finely grated
salt, grated nutmeg and freshly ground black pepper
2 eggs, beaten

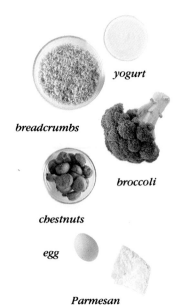

yogurt

breadcrumbs

broccoli

chestnuts

egg

Parmesan

1 Preheat the oven to 180°C/350°F/ Gas 4. Line a 900 g/2 lb loaf tin with non-stick baking paper.

2 Blanch or steam the broccoli for 3–4 minutes until just tender. Drain well. Reserve 1/4 of the smallest florets and chop the rest finely.

3 Mix together the chestnuts, breadcrumbs, yogurt and Parmesan, and season to taste.

4 Fold in the chopped broccoli, reserved florets and the beaten eggs.

5 Spoon the broccoli mixture into the prepared tin.

6 Place in a roasting tin and pour in boiling water to come halfway up the sides of the loaf tin. Bake for 20–25 minutes. Remove from the oven and tip out onto a plate or tray. Serve cut into even slices.

Guacamole with Crudités

This fresh-tasting spicy dip is made using peas instead of the traditional avocados.

Serves 4–6

INGREDIENTS
350 g/12 oz/2¼ cups frozen peas,
  defrosted
1 garlic clove, crushed
2 spring onions, trimmed and
  chopped
5 ml/1 tsp finely grated rind and juice
  of 1 lime
2.5 ml/½ tsp ground cumin
dash of Tabasco sauce
15 ml/1 tbsp reduced calorie
  mayonnaise
30 ml/2 tbsp chopped fresh coriander
salt and freshly ground black pepper
pinch of paprika and lime slices, to
  garnish

FOR THE CRUDITÉS
6 baby carrots
2 celery sticks
1 red-skinned eating apple
1 pear
15 ml/1 tbsp lemon or lime juice
6 baby sweetcorn

peas

vegetables

NUTRITIONAL NOTES

PER PORTION:

ENERGY 102Kcals/429KJ PROTEIN 4.83g
FAT 1.96g SATURATED FAT 0.22g
CARBOHYDRATE 17.1g
FIBRE 5.61g SUGAR 10g
SODIUM 54.8mg

1 Put the peas, garlic clove, spring onions, lime rind and juice, cumin, Tabasco sauce, mayonnaise and salt and freshly ground black pepper into a food processor or a blender for a few minutes and process until smooth.

2 Add the chopped coriander and process for a few more seconds. Spoon into a serving bowl, cover with clear film and chill in the refrigerator for 30 minutes, to let the flavours develop.

3 For the crudités, trim and peel the carrots. Halve the celery sticks lengthways and trim into sticks, the same length as the carrots. Quarter, core and thickly slice the apple and pear, then dip into the lemon or lime juice. Arrange with the baby sweetcorn on a platter.

4 Sprinkle the paprika over the guacamole and garnish with lime slices.

Cheese-stuffed Pears

These pears, with their scrumptious creamy topping, make a sublime dish when served with a simple salad.

Serves 4

INGREDIENTS
50 g/2 oz/¼ cup ricotta cheese
50 g/2 oz/¼ cup dolcelatte cheese
15 ml/1 tbsp honey
½ celery stick, finely sliced
8 green olives, pitted and roughly
  chopped
4 dates, stoned and cut into thin strips
pinch of paprika
4 ripe pears
150 ml/¼ pint/⅔ cup apple juice

honey

pear

apple juice

dates

dolcelatte

celery

olives

NUTRITIONAL NOTES
PER PORTION:

ENERGY 188.25Kcals/793KJ PROTEIN 4.67g
FAT 5.99g SATURATED FAT 3.28g
CARBOHYDRATE 30.69g
FIBRE 4.20g SUGAR 30.69g
SODIUM 180.75mg

1 Preheat the oven to 200°C/400°F/Gas 6. Place the ricotta in a bowl and crumble in the dolcelatte. Add the rest of the ingredients except for the pears and apple juice and mix well.

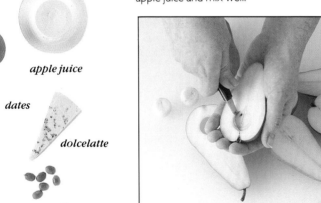

2 Halve the pears lengthwise and use a melon baller to remove the cores. Place in a ovenproof dish and divide the filling equally between them.

3 Pour in the apple juice and cover the dish with foil. Bake for 20 minutes or until the pears are tender.

4 Remove the foil and place the dish under a hot grill for 3 minutes. Serve immediately.

Aubergine, Roast Garlic and Red Pepper Pâté

This is a simple pâté of smoky baked aubergine, sweet pink peppercorns and red peppers, with more than a hint of garlic!

NUTRITIONAL NOTES

PER PORTION:

ENERGY 28Kcals/119KJ PROTEIN 1.63g
FAT 0.57g SATURATED FAT 0.13g
CARBOHYDRATE 4.54g
FIBRE 2.55g SUGAR 3.7g
SODIUM 5.25mg

Serves 4

INGREDIENTS
3 medium aubergines
2 red peppers
5 whole garlic cloves
7.5 ml/1½ tsp pink peppercorns in brine, drained and crushed
30 ml/2 tbsp chopped fresh coriander

aubergine

garlic

coriander

pink peppercorns

red pepper

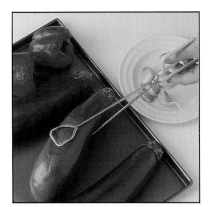

1 Preheat the oven to 200°C/400°F/Gas 6. Arrange the whole aubergines, peppers and garlic cloves on a baking sheet and place in the oven. After 10 minutes remove the garlic cloves and turn over the aubergines and peppers.

2 Peel the garlic cloves and place in the bowl of a blender.

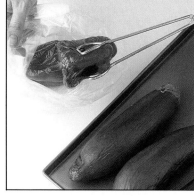

3 After a further 20 minutes remove the blistered and charred peppers from the oven and place in a plastic bag. Leave to cool.

4 After a further 10 minutes remove the aubergines from the oven. Split in half and scoop the flesh into a sieve placed over a bowl. Press the flesh with a spoon to remove the bitter juices.

5 Add the mixture to the garlic in the blender and blend until smooth. Place in a large mixing bowl.

6 Peel and chop the red peppers and stir into the aubergine mixture. Mix in the peppercorns and fresh coriander and serve at once.

Herby Fishcakes with Lemon and Chive Sauce

The wonderful flavour of fresh herbs makes these fishcakes the catch of the day.

Serves 4

INGREDIENTS
350 g/12 oz potatoes, peeled
75 ml/5 tbsp skimmed milk
350 g/12 oz haddock or hoki fillets, skinned
15 ml/1 tbsp lemon juice
15 ml/1 tbsp creamed horseradish sauce
30 ml/2 tbsp chopped fresh parsley
flour, for dusting
115 g/4 oz/2 cups fresh wholemeal breadcrumbs
salt and freshly ground black pepper
sprig of flat-leaf parsley, to garnish
mange tout and a sliced tomato and onion salad, to serve

FOR THE LEMON AND CHIVE SAUCE
thinly pared rind and juice of ½ small lemon
120 ml/4 fl oz/½ cup dry white wine
2 thin slices fresh root ginger
10 ml/2 tsp cornflour
30 ml/2 tbsp snipped fresh chives

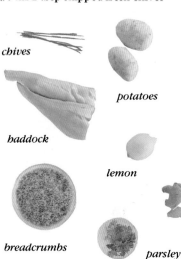

chives

potatoes

haddock

lemon

ginger

breadcrumbs

parsley

1 Cook the potatoes in a large saucepan of boiling water for 15-20 minutes. Drain and mash with the milk and season to taste.

2 Purée the fish together with the lemon juice and horseradish sauce in a blender or food processor. Mix together with the potatoes and parsley.

3 With floured hands, shape the mixture into eight fishcakes and coat with the breadcrumbs. Chill in the refrigerator for 30 minutes.

4 Cook the fishcakes under a pre-heated moderate grill for 5 minutes on each side, until browned.

5 To make the sauce, cut the lemon rind into julienne strips and put into a large saucepan together with the lemon juice, wine and ginger and season to taste.

NUTRITIONAL NOTES

Per portion:

ENERGY 266Kcals/1130KJ PROTEIN 27g
FAT 2.1g SATURATED FAT 0.4g
CARBOHYDRATE 32g
FIBRE 3.43g SUGAR 3.36g
SODIUM 289.7mg

6 Simmer uncovered for 6 minutes. Blend the cornflour with 15 ml/1 tbsp of cold water. Add to the saucepan and simmer until clear. Stir in the chives immediately before serving. Serve the sauce hot with the fishcakes, garnished with sprigs of flat-leaf parsley and accompanied with mange tout and a sliced tomato and onion salad.

Lemon Sole baked in a Paper Case

Make sure that these paper parcels are well sealed, so that none of the delicious juices can escape.

Serves 4

INGREDIENTS
4 lemon sole fillets, each weighing
    about 150 g/5 oz
½ small cucumber, sliced
4 lemon slices
60 ml/4 tbsp dry white wine
sprigs of fresh dill, to garnish
new potatoes and braised celery,
    to serve

FOR THE YOGURT HOLLANDAISE
150 ml/¼ pint natural low fat yogurt
5 ml/1 tsp lemon juice
2 egg yolks
5 ml/1 tsp Dijon mustard
salt and freshly ground black pepper

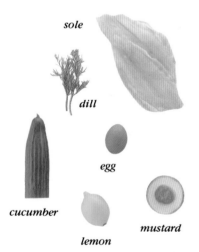

sole

dill

egg

cucumber

mustard

lemon

NUTRITIONAL NOTES
PER PORTION:

ENERGY 186Kcals/793KJ PROTEIN 29.5g
FAT 5.4g SATURATED FAT 1.25g
CARBOHYDRATE 3.16g
FIBRE 0.05g SUGAR 3.12g
SODIUM 216mg

1 Pre-heat the oven to 180°C/350°F/ Gas 4. Cut out four heart shapes from non-stick baking paper, each about 20 × 15 cm/8 × 6 in.

2 Place a sole fillet on one side of each heart. Arrange the cucumber and lemon slices on top of each fillet. Sprinkle with the wine and close the parcels by turning the edges of the paper and twisting to secure. Put on a baking tray and cook in the pre-heated oven for 15 minutes.

3 For the hollandaise, beat together the yogurt, lemon juice and egg yolks in a double boiler or bowl placed over a saucepan. Cook over simmering water, stirring for 15 minutes, or until thickened. (The sauce will become thinner after 10 minutes, but will thicken again.)

4 Remove from the heat and stir in the mustard. Season to taste with salt and freshly ground black pepper. Open the fish parcels, garnish with a sprig of dill and serve accompanied with the sauce, new potatoes and braised celery.

Plaice Provençal

Re-create the taste of the Mediterranean with this easy-to-make fish casserole.

Serves 4

INGREDIENTS
4 large plaice fillets
2 small red onions
120 ml/4 fl oz/½ cup vegetable stock
60 ml/4 tbsp dry red wine
1 garlic clove, crushed
2 courgettes, sliced
1 yellow pepper, seeded and sliced
400 g/14 oz can chopped tomatoes
15 ml/1 tbsp chopped fresh thyme
salt and freshly ground black pepper
potato gratin, to serve

chopped tomatoes

plaice

thyme

courgettes

red onion   *pepper*

NUTRITIONAL NOTES
PER PORTION:

ENERGY 167Kcals/710KJ PROTEIN 27.5g
FAT 2.55g SATURATED FAT 0.39g
CARBOHYDRATE 6.60g
FIBRE 1.6g SUGAR 6.3g
SODIUM 222mg

1 Pre-heat the oven to 180°C/350°F/ Gas 4. Skin the plaice with a sharp knife by laying it skin-side down. Holding the tail end, push the knife between the skin and flesh in a sawing movement. Hold the knife at a slight angle with the blade towards the skin.

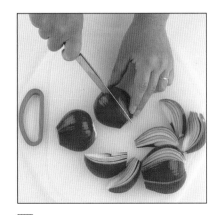

2 Cut each onion into eight wedges. Put into a heavy-based saucepan with the stock. Cover and simmer for 5 minutes. Uncover and continue to cook, stirring occasionally, until the stock has reduced entirely. Add the wine and garlic clove to the pan and continue to cook until the onions are soft.

3 Add the courgettes, yellow pepper, tomatoes and thyme and season to taste. Simmer for 3 minutes. Spoon the sauce into a large casserole.

4 Fold each fillet in half and place on top of the sauce. Cover and cook in the pre-heated oven for 15-20 minutes until the fish is opaque and cooked. Serve with potato gratin.

Smoked Trout Cannelloni

Smoked trout can be bought already filleted or whole.
If you buy fillets, you'll need 225 g/8 oz of fish.

Serves 4–6

INGREDIENTS
1 large onion, finely chopped
1 garlic clove, crushed
60 ml/4 tbsp vegetable stock
2 × 400 g/14 oz cans chopped
    tomatoes
2.5 ml/½ tsp dried mixed herbs
1 smoked trout, weighing about
    400 g/14 oz
75 g/3 oz/¾ cup frozen peas, thawed
75 g/3 oz/1½ cups fresh breadcrumbs
16 cannelloni tubes
salt and freshly ground black pepper
mixed salad, to serve

FOR THE CHEESE SAUCE
25 g/1 oz/2 tbsp low fat spread
25 g/1 oz/¼ cup plain flour
350 ml/12 fl oz/1½ cups
    skimmed milk
freshly grated nutmeg
15 g/½ oz/1½ tbsp freshly grated
    Parmesan cheese

mixed herbs

trout

onion

tomato

chopped tomatoes   *cannelloni*

1 Simmer the onion, garlic clove and stock in a large covered saucepan for 3 minutes. Uncover and continue to cook, stirring occasionally, until the stock has reduced entirely.

2 Stir in the tomatoes and dried herbs. Simmer uncovered for a further 10 minutes, or until very thick.

3 Meanwhile, skin the smoked trout with a sharp knife. Carefully flake the flesh and discard all the bones. Mix the fish together with the tomato mixture, peas, breadcrumbs, salt and freshly ground black pepper.

4 Pre-heat the oven to 190°C/375°F/ Gas 5. Spoon the filling into the cannelloni tubes and arrange in an ovenproof dish.

5 For the sauce, put the low fat spread, flour and milk into a saucepan and cook over a medium heat, whisking constantly until the sauce thickens. Simmer for 2-3 minutes, stirring all the time. Season to taste with salt, freshly ground black pepper and nutmeg.

NUTRITIONAL NOTES

Per portion:

ENERGY 277Kcals/1172KJ PROTEIN 17.83g
FAT 5.15g SATURATED FAT 1.1g
CARBOHYDRATE 42.3g
FIBRE 3.07g SUGAR 9.21g
SODIUM 259.3mg

COOK'S TIP

You can use a 220 g/7 oz can of tuna
in brine in place of the trout, if
preferred.

6 Pour the sauce over the cannelloni
and sprinkle with the grated Parmesan
cheese. Bake in the pre-heated oven for
35-40 minutes, or until the top is golden
and bubbling. Serve with a mixed salad.

Seafood Pasta Shells with Spinach Sauce

You'll need very large pasta shells, measuring about 4 cm/1½ in long for this dish; don't try stuffing smaller shells – they're much too fiddly!

NUTRITIONAL NOTES
Per portion:

ENERGY 363Kcals/1539KJ PROTEIN 34.94g
FAT 6.08g SATURATED FAT 2.09g
CARBOHYDRATE 45g
FIBRE 3.98g SUGAR 9.16g
SODIUM 622mg

Serves 4

INGREDIENTS
15 g/½ oz/1 tbsp low fat spread
8 spring onions, finely sliced
6 tomatoes
32 large dried pasta shells
225 g/8 oz/1 cup low fat soft cheese
90 ml/6 tbsp skimmed milk
pinch of freshly grated nutmeg
225 g/8 oz prawns
175 g/6 oz can white crabmeat,
   drained and flaked
115 g/4 oz frozen chopped spinach,
   thawed and drained
salt and freshly ground black pepper

spring onions

prawns

pasta shells

crabmeat

spinach

tomatoes

1 Pre-heat the oven to 150°C/300°F/Gas 2. Melt the low fat spread in a small saucepan and gently cook the spring onions for 3-4 minutes, or until softened.

2 Plunge the tomatoes into a saucepan of boiling water for 1 minute, then into a saucepan of cold water. Slip off the skins. Halve the tomatoes, remove the seeds and cores and roughly chop the flesh.

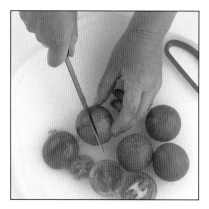

3 Cook the pasta shells in lightly salted boiling water for about 10 minutes, or until *al dente*. Drain well.

4 Put the low fat soft cheese and skimmed milk into a saucepan and heat gently, stirring until blended. Season with salt, freshly ground black pepper and a pinch of nutmeg. Measure 30 ml/2 tbsp of the sauce into a bowl.

5 Add the spring onions, tomatoes, prawns, and crabmeat to the bowl. Mix well. Spoon the filling into the shells and place in a single layer in a shallow ovenproof dish. Cover with foil and cook in the pre-heated oven for 10 minutes.

6 Stir the spinach into the remaining sauce. Bring to the boil and simmer gently for 1 minute, stirring all the time. Drizzle over the pasta shells and serve hot.

Cajun-style Cod

This recipe works equally well with any firm-fleshed fish such as swordfish, shark, tuna or halibut.

Serves 4

INGREDIENTS
4 cod steaks, each weighing about
   175 g/6 oz
30 ml/2 tbsp natural low fat yogurt
15 ml/1 tbsp lime or lemon juice
1 garlic clove, crushed
5 ml/1 tsp ground cumin
5 ml/1 tsp paprika
5 ml/1 tsp mustard powder
2.5 ml/½ tsp cayenne pepper
2.5 ml/½ tsp dried thyme
2.5 ml/½ tsp dried oregano
new potatoes and a mixed salad,
   to serve

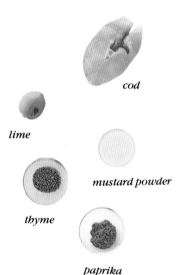

cod

lime

mustard powder

thyme

paprika

NUTRITIONAL NOTES
PER PORTION:

ENERGY 153Kcals/656KJ PROTEIN 33g
FAT 2.2g SATURATED FAT 0.3g
CARBOHYDRATE 1.81g
FIBRE 0.04g SUGAR 0.63g
SODIUM 114mg

1 Pat the fish dry on absorbent kitchen paper. Mix together the yogurt and lime or lemon juice and brush lightly over both sides of the fish.

2 Mix together the garlic clove, spices and herbs. Coat both sides of the fish with the seasoning mix, rubbing in well.

COOK'S TIP
If you don't have a ridged grill pan, heat several metal skewers under a grill until red hot. Holding the ends with a cloth, press onto the seasoned fish before cooking to give a ridged appearance.

3 Spray a ridged grill pan or heavy-based frying pan with non-stick cooking spray. Heat until very hot. Add the fish and cook over a high heat for 4 minutes, or until the underside is well browned.

4 Turn over and cook for a further 4 minutes, or until the steaks have cooked through. Serve immediately accompanied with new potatoes and a mixed salad.

Marinated Monkfish and Mussel Skewers

You can cook these fish kebabs on the barbecue – when the weather allows!

Serves 4

INGREDIENTS

450 g/1 lb monkfish, skinned and
  boned
5 ml/1 tsp olive oil
30 ml/2 tbsp lemon juice
5 ml/1 tsp paprika
1 garlic clove, crushed
4 turkey rashers
8 cooked mussels
8 raw prawns
15 ml/1 tbsp chopped fresh dill
salt and freshly ground black pepper
lemon wedges, to garnish
salad leaves and long-grain and wild
  rice, to serve

mussels

turkey rashers

dill

lemon

monkfish

NUTRITIONAL NOTES
PER PORTION:

ENERGY 159Kcals/674KJ PROTEIN 33.5g
FAT 2.52g SATURATED FAT 0.42g
CARBOHYDRATE 0.82g
FIBRE 0.13g SUGAR 0.16g
SODIUM 75mg

1 Cut the monkfish into 2.5 cm/1 in cubes and place in a shallow glass dish. Mix together the oil, lemon juice, paprika, and garlic clove and season with pepper.

2 Pour the marinade over the fish and toss to coat evenly. Cover and leave in a cool place for 30 minutes.

COOK'S TIP
Monkfish is ideal for kebabs, but can be expensive. Cod or hake are good alternatives.

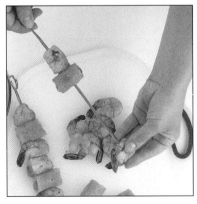

3 Cut the turkey rashers in half and wrap each strip around a mussel. Thread onto skewers alternating with the fish cubes and raw prawns.

4 Cook the kebabs under a hot grill for 7-8 minutes, turning once and basting with the marinade. Sprinkle with chopped dill and salt. Garnish with lemon wedges and serve with salad and rice.

Hot Spicy Prawns with Campanelle

Serves 4–6

INGREDIENTS

225 g/8 oz tiger prawns, cooked
  and peeled
1–2 garlic cloves, crushed
finely grated rind of 1 lemon
15 ml/1 tbsp lemon juice
1.5 ml/¼ tsp red chilli paste or large
  pinch dried ground chilli
15 ml/1 tbsp light soy sauce
150 g/5 oz smoked turkey rashers
1 shallot or small onion,
  finely chopped
60 ml/4 tbsp white wine
225 g/8 oz campanelle
60 ml/4 tbsp fish stock
4 firm ripe tomatoes, skinned,
  seeded and chopped
30 ml/2 tbsp chopped fresh parsley
salt and ground black pepper

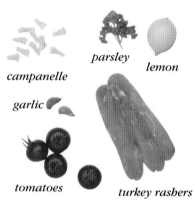

campanelle

parsley

lemon

garlic

tomatoes

turkey rashers

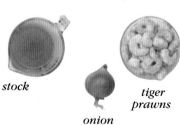

stock

onion

tiger prawns

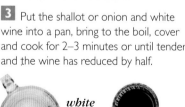

white wine

soy sauce

1 In a glass bowl, mix the prawns with the garlic, lemon rind and juice, chilli paste or ground chilli and soy sauce. Season with salt and pepper, cover and marinate the prawns for at least 1 hour.

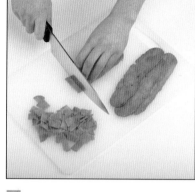

2 Grill the turkey rashers, then cut them into 5 mm/¼ in dice.

3 Put the shallot or onion and white wine into a pan, bring to the boil, cover and cook for 2–3 minutes or until tender and the wine has reduced by half.

4 Cook the campanelle in a large pan of boiling, salted water until *al dente*. Drain thoroughly.

5 Just before serving, put the prawns with their marinade into a large frying pan, bring to the boil quickly and add the smoked turkey and fish stock. Heat through for 1 minute.

6 Add to the pasta with the chopped tomatoes and parsley, toss quickly and serve immediately.

NUTRITIONAL NOTES
PER PORTION:

ENERGY 207Kcals/882KJ PROTEIN 17.5g
FAT 1.64g SATURATED FAT 0.25g
CARBOHYDRATE 31.2g
FIBRE 2.2g SUGAR 3.72g
SODIUM 314mg

Turkey and Tomato Hot-pot

Turkey is not just for festive occasions. Here, it's turned into tasty meatballs and simmered with rice in a tomato sauce.

Serves 4

INGREDIENTS
25 g/1 oz white bread, crusts removed
30 ml/2 tbsp skimmed milk
1 garlic clove, crushed
2.5 ml/½ tsp caraway seeds
225 g/8 oz minced turkey
1 egg white
350 ml/12 fl oz/1½ cups chicken stock
400 g/14 oz can plum tomatoes
15 ml/1 tbsp tomato purée
90 g/3½ oz/½ cup easy-cook rice
salt and freshly ground black pepper
15 ml/1 tbsp chopped fresh basil, to garnish
carrot and courgette ribbons, to serve

minced turkey

basil

rice

bread

tomato purée

plum tomatoes

caraway seeds

garlic

COOK'S TIP
To make carrot and courgette ribbons, cut the vegetables lengthways into thin strips using a vegetable peeler, and blanch or steam until cooked through.

1 Cut the bread into small cubes and put into a mixing bowl. Sprinkle over the milk and leave to soak for 5 minutes.

2 Add the garlic clove, caraway seeds, turkey, salt and freshly ground black pepper to the bread. Mix together well.

3 Whisk the egg white until stiff, then fold, half at a time, into the turkey mixture. Chill for 10 minutes in the refrigerator.

4 Put the stock, tomatoes and tomato purée into a large, heavy-based saucepan and bring to the boil.

5 Add the rice, stir and cook briskly for about 5 minutes. Turn the heat down to a gentle simmer.

6 Meanwhile, shape the turkey mixture into 16 small balls. Carefully drop them into the tomato stock and simmer for a further 8-10 minutes, or until the turkey balls and rice are cooked. Garnish with chopped basil, and serve with carrot and courgette ribbons.

Turkey Tonnato

This low fat version of the Italian dish 'vitello tonnato' is garnished with fine strips of red pepper instead of the traditional anchovy fillets.

NUTRITIONAL NOTES
Per portion:

ENERGY 239Kcals/1004KJ PROTEIN 38.45g
FAT 7.55g SATURATED FAT 0.69g
CARBOHYDRATE 4.45g
FIBRE 0.58g SUGAR 3.2g
SODIUM 414mg

Serves 4

INGREDIENTS

450 g/1 lb turkey fillets
1 small onion, sliced
1 bay leaf
4 black peppercorns
350 ml/12 fl oz/1½ cups chicken stock
200 g/7 oz can tuna in brine, drained
75 ml/5 tbsp reduced calorie mayonnaise
30 ml/2 tbsp lemon juice
2 red peppers, seeded and thinly sliced
about 25 capers, drained
pinch of salt
mixed salad and tomatoes, to serve

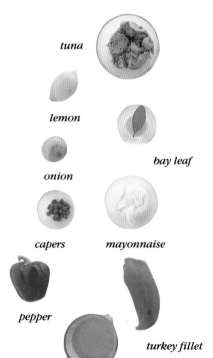

tuna

lemon

onion

bay leaf

capers

mayonnaise

pepper

turkey fillet

stock

1 Put the turkey fillets in a single layer in a large, heavy-based saucepan. Add the onion, bay leaf, peppercorns and stock. Bring to the boil and reduce the heat. Cover and simmer for 12 minutes, or until tender.

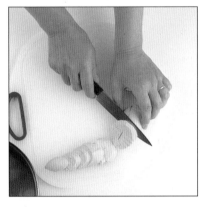

2 Turn off the heat and leave the turkey to cool in the stock, then remove with a slotted spoon. Slice thickly and arrange on a serving plate.

3 Boil the stock until reduced to about 75 ml/5 tbsp. Strain and leave to cool.

4 Put the tuna, mayonnaise, lemon juice, 45 ml/3 tbsp of the reduced stock and salt into a blender or food processor and purée until smooth.

5 Stir in enough of the remaining stock to reduce the sauce to the thickness of double cream. Spoon over the turkey.

6 Arrange the strips of red pepper in a lattice pattern over the turkey. Put a caper in the centre of each square. Chill in the refrigerator for 1 hour and serve with a fresh mixed salad and tomatoes.

Chicken with Orange and Mustard Sauce

The beauty of this recipe is its simplicity; the chicken continues to cook in its own juices while you prepare the sauce.

Serves 4

INGREDIENTS
2 large oranges
4 chicken breasts, boned and skinned
5 ml/1 tsp sunflower oil
salt and freshly ground black pepper
new potatoes and sliced courgettes
   tossed in parsley, to serve

FOR THE ORANGE AND MUSTARD SAUCE
10 ml/2 tsp cornflour
150 ml/¼ pint/⅔ cup strained yogurt
5 ml/1 tsp Dijon mustard

chicken breast

yogurt

cornflour

mustard

orange

NUTRITIONAL NOTES
PER PORTION:

ENERGY 263Kcals/1120KJ PROTEIN 44.5g
FAT 4.61g SATURATED FAT 1.13g
CARBOHYDRATE 12.03g
FIBRE 1.36g SUGAR 9.71g
SODIUM 145mg

1 Peel the oranges using a sharp knife, removing all the white pith. Remove the segments by cutting between the membranes, holding the fruit over a small bowl to catch any juice. Set aside with the juice until required.

2 Season the chicken with salt and freshly ground black pepper. Heat the oil in a non-stick frying pan and cook the chicken for 5 minutes on each side. Take out of the frying pan and wrap in foil; the meat will continue to cook for a while.

3 For the sauce, blend together the cornflour with the juice from the orange. Add the yogurt and mustard. Put into the frying pan and slowly bring to the boil. Simmer for 1 minute.

4 Add the orange segments to the sauce and heat gently. Unwrap the chicken and add any excess juices to the sauce. Slice on the diagonal and serve with the sauce, new potatoes and sliced courgettes tossed in parsley.

Stir-fried Beef and Broccoli

This spicy beef may be served with noodles or on a bed of boiled rice for a speedy and low calorie Chinese meal.

Serves 4

INGREDIENTS

350 g/12 oz rump or lean prime
   casserole steak
15 ml/1 tbsp cornflour
5 ml/1 tsp sesame oil
350 g/12 oz broccoli, cut into
   small florets
4 spring onions, sliced on the diagonal
1 carrot, cut into matchstick strips
1 garlic clove, crushed
2.5 cm/1 in piece root ginger, cut into
   very fine strips
120 ml/4 fl oz/½ cup beef stock
30 ml/2 tbsp soy sauce
30 ml/2 tbsp dry sherry
10 ml/2 tsp soft light brown sugar
spring onion tassels, to garnish
noodles or rice, to serve

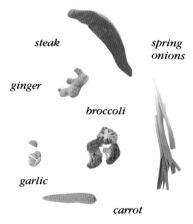

steak

spring onions

ginger

broccoli

garlic

carrot

NUTRITIONAL NOTES

PER PORTION:

ENERGY 200Kcals/841KJ PROTEIN 24.5g
FAT 5.88g SATURATED FAT 1.89g
CARBOHYDRATE 10.64g
FIBRE 2.97g SUGAR 5.8g
SODIUM 171mg

1 Trim the beef and cut into thin slices across the grain. Cut each slice into thin strips. Toss in the cornflour to coat thoroughly.

2 Heat the sesame oil in a large non-stick frying pan or wok. Add the beef strips and stir-fry over a brisk heat for 3 minutes. Remove and set aside.

COOK'S TIP

To make spring onion tassels, trim the bulb base then cut the green shoot so that the onion is 7.5 cm/3 in long. Shred to within 2.5 cm/1 in of the base and put into iced water for 1 hour.

3 Add the broccoli, spring onions, carrot, garlic clove, ginger and stock to the frying pan or wok. Cover and simmer for 3 minutes. Uncover and cook, stirring until all the stock has reduced entirely.

4 Mix the soy sauce, sherry and brown sugar together. Add to the frying pan or wok with the beef. Cook for 2–3 minutes stirring continuously. Spoon into a warm serving dish and garnish with spring onion tassels. Serve on a bed of noodles or rice.

Hot and Sour Pork

Chinese five-spice powder is made from a mixture of ground star anise, Szechuan pepper, cassia, cloves and fennel seed and has a flavour similar to liquorice. If you can't find any, use mixed spice instead.

NUTRITIONAL NOTES

PER PORTION:

ENERGY 194.25Kcals/815.25KJ PROTEIN 21.04g
FAT 7.39g SATURATED FAT 2.22g
CARBOHYDRATE 11.36g
FIBRE 0.82g SUGAR 7.87g
SODIUM 366mg

Serves 4

INGREDIENTS
350 g/12 oz pork fillet
5 ml/1 tsp sunflower oil
2.5 cm/1 in piece root ginger, grated
1 red chilli, seeded and finely chopped
5 ml/1 tsp Chinese five-spice powder
15 ml/1 tbsp sherry vinegar
15 ml/1 tbsp soy sauce
225 g/8 oz can pineapple chunks in natural juice
175 ml/6 fl oz/¾ cup chicken stock
20 ml/4 tsp cornflour
1 small green pepper, seeded and sliced
115 g/4 oz baby sweetcorn, halved
salt and freshly ground black pepper
sprig of flat-leaf parsley, to garnish
boiled rice, to serve

pineapple chunks

pork fillet

chilli

cornflour

soy sauce

pepper

baby sweetcorn

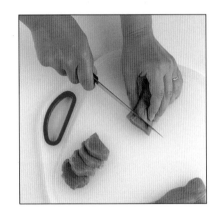

1 Pre-heat the oven to 160°C/325°F/Gas 3. Trim away any visible fat from the pork and cut into 1 cm/½ in thick slices.

2 Brush the sunflower oil over the base of a flameproof casserole. Heat over a medium flame, then fry the meat for about 2 minutes on each side or until lightly browned.

3 Blend together the ginger, chilli, five-spice powder, vinegar and soy sauce.

4 Drain the pineapple chunks, reserving the juice. Make the stock up to 300 ml/½ pint/1¼ cups with the reserved juice, mix together with the spices and pour over the pork.

5 Slowly bring to the boil. Blend the cornflour with 15 ml/1 tbsp of cold water and gradually stir into the pork. Add the vegetables and season to taste.

6 Cover and cook in the oven for 30 minutes. Stir in the pineapple and cook for a further 5 minutes. Garnish with flat-leaf parsley and serve with boiled rice.

Honey-roast Pork with Thyme and Rosemary

Herbs and honey add flavour and sweetness to tenderloin – the leanest cut of pork.

NUTRITIONAL NOTES

Per portion:

ENERGY 248.75Kcals/1043.25KJ PROTEIN 26.15g
FAT 8.12g SATURATED FAT 2.63g
CARBOHYDRATE 16.42g
FIBRE 0.87g SUGAR 14.54g
SODIUM 284.5mg

Serves 4

INGREDIENTS
450 g/1 lb pork tenderloin
30 ml/2 tbsp thick honey
30 ml/2 tbsp Dijon mustard
5 ml/1 tsp chopped fresh rosemary
2.5 ml/½ tsp chopped fresh thyme
¼ tsp whole tropical peppercorns
sprigs of fresh rosemary and thyme, to
    garnish
potato gratin and cauliflower,
    to serve

FOR THE RED ONION CONFIT
4 red onions
350 ml/12 fl oz/1½ cups
    vegetable stock
15 ml/1 tbsp red wine vinegar
15 ml/1 tbsp caster sugar
1 garlic clove, crushed
30 ml/2 tbsp ruby port
pinch of salt

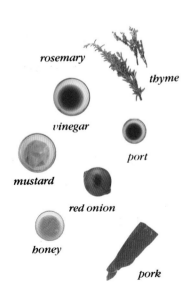

rosemary

thyme

vinegar

port

mustard

red onion

honey

pork

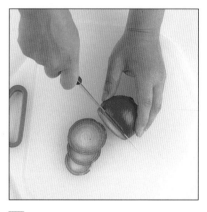

1 Pre-heat the oven to 180°C/350°F/ Gas 4. Trim off any visible fat from the pork. Put the honey, mustard, rosemary and thyme in a small bowl and mix them together well.

2 Crush the peppercorns using a pestle and mortar. Spread the honey mixture over the pork and sprinkle with the crushed peppercorns. Place in a non-stick roasting tin and cook in the pre-heated oven for 35-45 minutes.

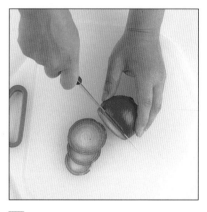

3 For the red onion confit, slice the onions into rings and put them into a heavy-based saucepan.

4 Add the stock, vinegar, sugar and garlic clove to the saucepan. Bring to the boil, then reduce the heat. Cover and simmer for 15 minutes.

5 Uncover and pour in the port and continue to simmer, stirring occasionally, until the onions are soft and the juices thick and syrupy. Season to taste with salt.

6 Cut the pork into slices and arrange on four warmed plates. Serve garnished with rosemary and thyme and accompanied with the red onion confit, potato gratin and cauliflower.

Spiced Vegetables with Coconut

This spicy and substantial dish could be served as a starter, or as a vegetarian main course for two. Eat it with spoons and forks, and hunks of granary bread for mopping up the delicious coconut milk.

Serves 2–4 as a starter

INGREDIENTS
1 red chilli
2 large carrots
6 stalks celery
1 bulb fennel
30 ml/2 tbsp grapeseed oil
2.5 cm/1 in piece root ginger, peeled and grated
1 clove garlic, crushed
3 spring onions, sliced
1 × 400 ml/14 fl oz can thin coconut milk
15 ml/1 tbsp fresh coriander, chopped
salt and freshly ground black pepper
coriander sprigs, to garnish

celery

spring onions

fennel

carrot

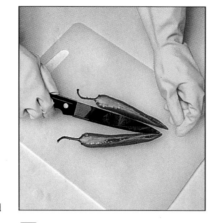

1 Halve, deseed and finely chop the chilli. If necessary, wear rubber gloves to protect your hands.

2 Slice the carrots on the diagonal. Slice the celery stalks on the diagonal.

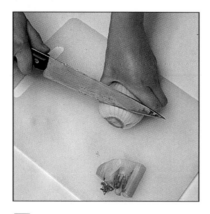

3 Trim the fennel head and slice roughly, using a sharp knife.

4 Heat the wok, then add the oil. When the oil is hot, add the ginger and garlic, chilli, carrots, celery, fennel and spring onions and stir-fry for 2 minutes.

5 Stir in the coconut milk with a large spoon and bring to the boil.

6 Stir in the coriander and salt and pepper, and serve garnished with coriander sprigs.

Curried Chicken Salad

Serves 4

INGREDIENTS
2 cooked chicken breasts, boned
175 g/6 oz French beans
350 g/12 oz multi-coloured penne
150 ml/¼ pint/⅔ cup low-fat yogurt
5 ml/1 tsp mild curry powder
1 garlic clove, crushed
1 green chilli, seeded and
    finely chopped
30 ml/2 tbsp chopped
    fresh coriander
4 firm ripe tomatoes, skinned,
    seeded and cut in strips
salt and ground black pepper
coriander leaves, to garnish

multi-coloured penne

chicken breasts

French beans

green chilli

coriander

tomatoes

low-fat yogurt

garlic

1 Remove the skin from the chicken and cut in strips. Cut the green beans in 2.5 cm/1 in lengths and cook in boiling water for 5 minutes. Drain and rinse under cold water.

2 Cook the pasta in a large pan of boiling, salted water until *al dente*. Drain and rinse thoroughly.

NUTRITIONAL NOTES
PER PORTION:

ENERGY 448.75Kcals/1906.5KJ PROTEIN 34.9g
FAT 4.14g SATURATED FAT 0.7g
CARBOHYDRATE 72.61g
FIBRE 4.88g SUGAR 9.24g
SODIUM 92mg

3 To make the sauce, mix the yogurt, curry powder, garlic, chilli and chopped coriander together in a bowl. Stir in the chicken pieces and leave to stand for 30 minutes.

4 Transfer the pasta to a glass bowl and toss with the beans and tomatoes. Spoon over the chicken and sauce. Garnish with coriander leaves.

Lentil and Cabbage Salad

This warm crunchy salad makes a satisfying meal if served with crusty French bread or wholemeal rolls.

Serves 4–6

INGREDIENTS
225 g/8 oz/1 cup puy lentils
1 garlic clove
1 bay leaf
1 small onion, peeled and studded
  with 2 cloves
15 ml/1 tbsp olive oil
1 red onion, finely sliced
2 garlic cloves, crushed
15 ml/1 tbsp thyme leaves
350 g/12 oz cabbage, finely shredded
finely grated rind and juice of 1 lemon
15 ml/1 tbsp raspberry vinegar
salt and freshly ground black pepper

NUTRITIONAL NOTES
PER PORTION:

ENERGY 157.33Kcals/664.83KJ PROTEIN 10.2g
FAT 3.41g SATURATED FAT 0.44g
CARBOHYDRATE 23.03g
FIBRE 4.04g SUGAR 4.1g

thyme *cabbage*

onion

red onion

bay leaf

lemon

garlic

cloves *peppercorns*

1 Rinse the lentils in cold water and place in a large pan with 1.3 litres/ 2¼ pints/6 cups cold water, peeled garlic clove, bay leaf and clove-studded onion. Bring to the boil and cook for 10 minutes. Reduce the heat, cover and simmer gently for 15-20 minutes. Drain; remove the onion, garlic and bay leaf.

2 Heat the oil in a large pan. Add the red onion, garlic and thyme and cook for 5 minutes until softened.

3 Add the cabbage and cook for 3–5 minutes until just cooked but still crunchy.

4 Stir in the cooked lentils, lemon rind and juice and the raspberry vinegar. Season to taste and serve.

Fruit and Fibre Salad

Fresh, fast and filling, this salad makes a great starter,
supper or snack.

Serves 4–6

INGREDIENTS
225 g/8 oz red or white cabbage or a
mixture of both
3 medium carrots
1 pear
1 red-skinned eating apple
200 g/7 oz can green flageolet beans,
drained
50 g/2 oz/¼ cup chopped dates

FOR THE DRESSING
2.5 ml/½ tsp dry English mustard
10 ml/2 tsp clear honey
30 ml/2 tbsp orange juice
5 ml/1 tsp white wine vinegar
2.5 ml/½ tsp paprika
salt and freshly ground black pepper

carrot
dates
orange
flageolet beans
cabbage
pear
apple

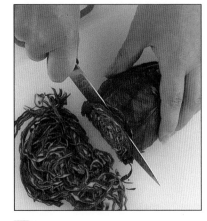

1 Shred the cabbage very finely, discarding any tough stalks.

2 Cut the carrots into very thin strips, about 5 cm/2 in long.

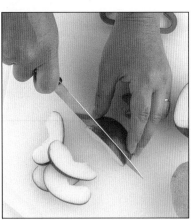

3 Quarter, core and slice the pear and apple, leaving the skin on.

4 Put the fruit and vegetables in a bowl with the beans and dates. Mix well.

5 For the dressing, blend the mustard with the honey until smooth. Add the orange juice, vinegar, paprika and seasoning and mix well.

NUTRITIONAL NOTES

Per portion:

ENERGY 84.17Kcals/356.16KJ PROTEIN 3.13g
FAT 0.52g SATURATED FAT 0.075g
CARBOHYDRATE 17.66g
FIBRE 4.08g SUGAR 13.3g
SODIUM 152.5mg

6 Pour the dressing over the salad and toss to coat. Chill in the refrigerator for 30 minutes before serving.

Marinated Cucumber Salad

Sprinkling the cucumber with salt draws out some of the water and makes them crisper.

Serves 4–6

INGREDIENTS
2 medium cucumbers
15 ml/1 tbsp salt
90 g/3½ oz/½ cup granulated sugar
175 ml/6 fl oz/¾ cup dry cider
15 ml/1 tbsp cider vinegar
45 ml/3 tbsp chopped fresh dill
pinch of pepper

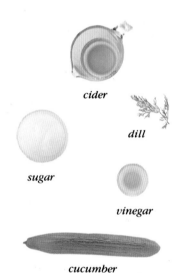

cider

dill

sugar

vinegar

cucumber

NUTRITIONAL NOTES

Per portion:

ENERGY 74Kcals/313KJ PROTEIN 0.4g
FAT 0.07g SATURATED FAT 0g
CARBOHYDRATE 16.8g
FIBRE 0.28g SUGAR 16.8g
SODIUM 333mg

1 Slice the cucumbers thinly and place them in a colander, sprinkling salt between each layer. Put the colander over a bowl and leave to drain for 1 hour.

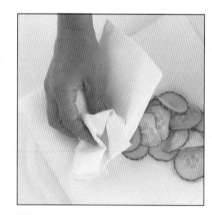

2 Thoroughly rinse the cucumber under cold running water to remove excess salt, then pat dry on absorbent kitchen paper.

3 Gently heat the sugar, cider and vinegar in a saucepan, until the sugar has dissolved. Remove from the heat and leave to cool. Put the cucumber slices in a bowl, pour over the cider mixture and leave to marinate for 2 hours.

4 Drain the cucumber and sprinkle with the dill and pepper to taste. Mix well and transfer to a serving dish. Chill in the refrigerator until ready to serve.

Carrot, Raisin and Apricot Coleslaw

A tasty high fibre coleslaw, combining cabbage, carrots and dried fruit in a light yogurt dressing.

Serves 6

INGREDIENTS
350 g/12 oz/3 cups white cabbage, finely shredded
225 g/8 oz/1½ cups carrots, coarsely grated
1 red onion, sliced
3 celery sticks, sliced
175 g/6 oz/1 cup raisins
75 g/3 oz ready-to-eat dried apricots, chopped
120 ml/8 tbsp reduced-calorie mayonnaise
90 ml/6 tbsp low-fat plain yogurt
30 ml/2 tbsp chopped fresh mixed herbs
salt and ground black pepper

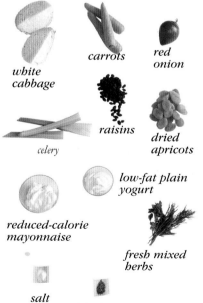

white cabbage

carrots

red onion

raisins

dried apricots

celery

low-fat plain yogurt

reduced-calorie mayonnaise

fresh mixed herbs

salt

black pepper

1 Put the cabbage and carrot in a large bowl.

2 Add the onion, celery, raisins and apricots and mix well.

NUTRITIONAL NOTES
PER PORTION:

ENERGY 195Kcals/822KJ PROTEIN 3.3g
FAT 6g SATURATED FAT 0.11g
CARBOHYDRATE 33g
FIBRE 3.65g SUGAR 32g
SODIUM 241mg

3 In a small bowl, mix together the mayonnaise, yogurt, herbs and seasoning.

COOK'S TIP
Use other dried fruit such as sultanas and ready-to-eat dried pears or peaches in place of the raisins and apricots.

4 Add the mayonnaise dressing to the bowl and toss the ingredients together to mix. Cover and chill for several hours before serving.

Vegetables à la Grecque

This simple side salad is made with winter vegetables, but you can vary it according to the season.

Serves 4

INGREDIENTS

175 ml/6 fl oz/¾ cup white wine
5 ml/1 tsp olive oil
30 ml/2 tbsp lemon juice
2 bay leaves
sprig of fresh thyme
4 juniper berries
450 g/1 lb leeks, trimmed and cut into
    2.5 cm/1 in lengths
1 small cauliflower, broken into
    florets
4 celery sticks, sliced on the diagonal
30 ml/2 tbsp chopped fresh parsley
salt and freshly ground black pepper

wine

celery

cauliflower

parsley

olive oil

leeks

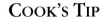

NUTRITIONAL NOTES
PER PORTION:

ENERGY 88.25Kcals/349KJ PROTEIN 3.61g
FAT 2.32g SATURATED FAT 0.37g
CARBOHYDRATE 5.32g
FIBRE 3.86g SUGAR 4.23g
SODIUM 28mg

1 Put the wine, oil, lemon juice, bay leaves, thyme and juniper berries into a large, heavy-based saucepan and bring to the boil. Cover and leave to simmer for 20 minutes.

2 Add the leeks, cauliflower and celery. Simmer very gently for 5–6 minutes or until just tender.

COOK'S TIP
Choose a dry or medium-dry white wine for this dish.

3 Remove the vegetables with a slotted spoon and transfer them to a serving dish. Briskly boil the cooking liquid for 15-20 minutes, or until reduced by half. Strain.

4 Stir the parsley into the liquid and season to taste. Pour over the vegetables and leave to cool. Chill in the refrigerator for at least 1 hour before serving.

Tabbouleh with Fennel and Pomegranate

A fresh salad originating in the Middle East, with the added crunchiness of fennel and sweet pomegranate seeds. It is perfect for a summer lunch.

Serves 6

INGREDIENTS
225 g/8 oz/1 cup bulgur wheat
2 fennel bulbs
1 small fresh red chilli, seeded and
    finely chopped
1 celery stick, finely sliced
30 ml/2 tbsp olive oil
finely grated rind and juice of 2
    lemons
6–8 spring onions, chopped
90 ml/6 tbsp chopped fresh mint
90 ml/6 tbsp chopped fresh parsley
1 pomegranate, seeds removed
salt and freshly ground black pepper

lemon

red chilli

celery

bulgur wheat

spring
onion

fennel

pomegranate

parsley

mint

1 Place the bulgur wheat in a bowl and pour over enough cold water to cover. Leave to stand for 30 minutes.

2 Drain the wheat through a sieve, pressing out any excess water.

NUTRITIONAL NOTES
PER PORTION:
ENERGY 209.66Kcals/876.5KJ PROTEIN 5.6g
FAT 6.12g SATURATED FAT 0.73g
CARBOHYDRATE 34g
FIBRE 2.26g SUGAR 4.48g
SODIUM 16mg

3 Halve the fennel bulbs and cut into very fine slices.

4 Mix all the remaining ingredients together, including the soaked bulgur wheat and fennel. Season well, cover, and set aside for 30 minutes before serving.

Carrot Mousse with Mushroom Sauce

The combination of fresh vegetables in this impressive yet easy-to-make mousse makes healthy eating a pleasure.

Serves 4

NUTRITIONAL NOTES
PER PORTION:

ENERGY 179.75Kcals/753.25KJ PROTEIN 13.43g
FAT 6.53g SATURATED FAT 1.85g
CARBOHYDRATE 17.77g
FIBRE 2.81g SUGAR 11.29g
SODIUM 170.73mg

INGREDIENTS

350 g/12 oz carrots, roughly chopped
1 small red pepper, seeded and
    roughly chopped
45 ml/3 tbsp vegetable stock or water
2 eggs
1 egg white
115 g/4 oz/½ cup quark or low fat soft
    cheese
15 ml/1 tbsp chopped fresh tarragon
salt and freshly ground black pepper
sprig of fresh tarragon, to garnish
boiled rice and leeks, to serve

FOR THE MUSHROOM SAUCE

25 g/1 oz/2 tbsp low fat spread
175 g/6 oz mushrooms, sliced
30 ml/2 tbsp plain flour
250 ml/8 fl oz/1 cup skimmed milk

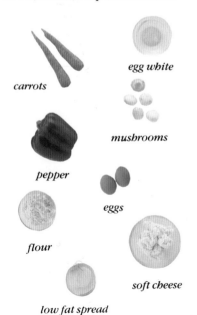

carrots

egg white

mushrooms

pepper

eggs

flour

soft cheese

low fat spread

1 Pre-heat the oven to 190°C/375°F/ Gas 5. Line the bases of four 150 ml/ ¼ pint/⅔ cup dariole moulds or ramekin dishes with non-stick baking paper. Put the carrots and red pepper in a small saucepan with the vegetable stock or water. Cover and cook for 5 minutes, or until tender. Drain well.

2 Lightly beat the eggs and egg white together. Mix with the quark or low fat soft cheese. Season to taste. Purée the cooked vegetables in a food processor or blender. Add the cheese mixture and process for a few seconds more until smooth. Stir in the chopped tarragon.

3 Divide the carrot mixture between the prepared dariole moulds or ramekin dishes and cover with foil. Place the dishes in a roasting tin half-filled with hot water. Bake in the pre-heated oven for 35 minutes, or until set.

4 For the mushroom sauce, melt 15 g/½ oz/1 tbsp of the low fat spread in a frying pan. Add the mushrooms and gently sauté for 5 minutes, until soft.

5 Put the remaining low fat spread in a small saucepan together with the flour and milk. Cook over a medium heat, stirring all the time, until the sauce thickens. Stir in the mushrooms and season to taste.

6 Turn out each mousse onto a serving plate. Spoon over a little sauce and serve the remainder separately. Garnish with a sprig of fresh tarragon and serve with boiled rice and leeks.

Cheese and Onion Slice

This inexpensive supper dish is made substantial with the addition of porridge oats.

Serves 6

INGREDIENTS
2 large onions, thinly sliced
1 garlic clove, crushed
150 ml/¼ pint/⅔ cup vegetable stock
5 ml/1 tsp vegetable extract
250 g/9 oz/3 cups porridge oats
115 g/4 oz/1 cup grated Edam cheese
30 ml/2 tbsp chopped fresh parsley
2 eggs, lightly beaten
1 medium potato, peeled
salt and freshly ground black pepper
coleslaw and tomatoes, halved,
    to serve

porridge oats

Edam cheese

eggs

parsley

onion

potato

NUTRITIONAL NOTES
PER PORTION:

ENERGY 287.7Kcals/1210.5KJ PROTEIN 13.61g
FAT 10.83g SATURATED FAT 3.67g
CARBOHYDRATE 36.17g
FIBRE 3.66g SUGAR 1.21g
SODIUM 241.67mg

1 Pre-heat the oven to 180°C/350°F/Gas 4. Line the base of a 20 cm/8 in sandwich tin with non-stick baking paper. Put the onions, garlic clove and stock into a heavy-based saucepan and simmer until the stock has reduced entirely. Stir in the vegetable extract.

2 Spread the oats on a baking sheet and toast in the oven for 10 minutes. Mix with the onions, cheese, parsley, eggs, salt and freshly ground black pepper.

3 Thinly slice the potato and use it to line the base of the tin. Spoon in the oat mixture. Cover with a piece of foil.

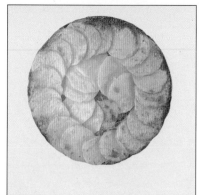

4 Bake in the pre-heated oven for 35 minutes. Turn out onto a baking sheet and remove the lining paper. Put under a pre-heated hot grill to brown the potatoes. Cut into wedges and serve hot with coleslaw and halved tomatoes.

Leek and Caraway Gratin

Tender leeks are mixed with a creamy caraway sauce and a crunchy carrot topping.

Serves 4–6

INGREDIENTS

675 g/1½ lb leeks, cut into chunks
150 ml/¼ pint/⅔ cup vegetable stock
45 ml/3 tbsp dry white wine
5 ml/1 tsp caraway seeds
pinch of salt
275 ml/10 fl oz skimmed milk as required
25 g/1 oz/2 tbsp polyunsaturated margarine
25 g/1 oz/¼ cup plain flour
115 g/4 oz/2 cups fresh wholemeal breadcrumbs
115 g/4 oz/ 2 cups grated carrot
30 ml/ 2 tbsp chopped fresh parsley
75 g/3 oz Jarlsberg cheese, grated
25 g/1 oz/2 tbsp slivered almonds

NUTRITIONAL NOTES

PER PORTION:

ENERGY 193.83Kcals/813KJ PROTEIN 10.85g
FAT 8.52g SATURATED FAT 2.04g
CARBOHYDRATE 18.75g
FIBRE 4.73g SUGAR 6.93g
SODIUM 168.33mg

parsley

vegetable stock

Jarlsberg

breadcrumbs

leek

butter

1 Place the leeks in a large pan. Add the vegetable stock, wine, caraway seeds and salt. Bring to a simmer, cover and cook for 5–7 minutes until the leeks are just tender.

2 With a slotted spoon, transfer the leeks to an ovenproof dish. Reduce the remaining liquid to half then make the amount up to 350 ml/12 fl oz/1½ cups with skimmed milk.

3 Preheat the oven to 180°C/350°F/ Gas 4. Melt the margarine in a saucepan, stir in the flour and cook without allowing it to colour for 1–2 minutes. Gradually add the stock and milk, stirring well, until you have a smooth sauce. Simmer for 5–6 minutes then pour over the leeks in the dish.

4 Mix together the breadcrumbs, carrot, parsley, Jarlsberg cheese and slivered almonds in a bowl and sprinkle over the leeks. Bake for 20–25 minutes until golden.

Vegetarian Cassoulet

Every town in south-west France has its own version of this popular classic. Warm French bread is all that is needed to complete this hearty vegetable version.

Serves 4–6

INGREDIENTS
400 g/14 oz/2 cups dried
 haricot beans
1 bay leaf
2 onions
3 whole cloves
2 garlic cloves, crushed
5 ml/1 tsp olive oil
2 leeks, thickly sliced
12 baby carrots
115 g/4 oz button mushrooms
400 g/14 oz can chopped tomatoes
15 ml/1 tbsp tomato purée
5 ml/1 tsp paprika
15 ml/1 tbsp chopped fresh thyme
30 ml/2 tbsp chopped fresh parsley
115 g/4 oz/2 cups fresh white
 breadcrumbs
salt and freshly ground black pepper

1 Soak the beans overnight in plenty of cold water. Drain and rinse under cold running water. Put them in a saucepan together with 1.75 litres/3 pints/7½ cups of cold water and the bay leaf. Bring to the boil and cook rapidly for 10 minutes.

2 Peel one of the onions and spike with cloves. Add to the beans and reduce the heat. Cover and simmer gently for 1 hour, until the beans are almost tender. Drain, reserving the stock but discarding the bay leaf and onion.

3 Chop the remaining onion and put it into a large flameproof casserole together with the garlic cloves and olive oil. Cook gently for 5 minutes, or until softened.

chopped tomatoes　　*bay leaf*

leek

breadcrumbs

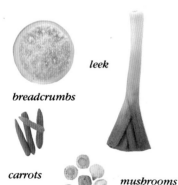

carrots　　*mushrooms*

4 Pre-heat the oven to 160°C/325°F/ Gas 3. Add the leeks, carrots, mushrooms, chopped tomatoes, tomato purée, paprika, thyme and 400 ml/ 14 fl oz/1⅔ cups of the reserved stock to the casserole.

5 Bring to the boil, cover and simmer gently for 10 minutes. Stir in the cooked beans and parsley. Season to taste.

NUTRITIONAL NOTES
PER PORTION:

ENERGY 305.5Kcals/1296KJ PROTEIN 18.8g
FAT 3.33g SATURATED FAT 0.58g
CARBOHYDRATE 53.3g
FIBRE 16.33g SUGAR 12.16g
SODIUM 208.66mg

6 Sprinkle with the breadcrumbs and bake uncovered in the pre-heated oven for 35 minutes, or until the topping is golden brown and crisp.

Mushroom and Okra Curry with Fresh Mango Relish

This simple but delicious curry with its fresh gingery mango relish is best served with plain basmati rice.

Serves 4

INGREDIENTS
4 garlic cloves, roughly chopped
2.5 cm/1 in piece of fresh ginger root, peeled and roughly chopped
1–2 red chillies, seeded and chopped
175 ml/6 fl oz/¾ cup cold water
15 ml/1 tbsp sunflower oil
5 ml/1 tsp coriander seeds
5 ml/1 tsp cumin seeds
5 ml/1 tsp ground cumin
2 green cardamom pods, seeds removed and ground
pinch of ground turmeric
1 × 400 g/14 oz can chopped tomatoes
450 g/1 lb mushrooms, quartered if large
225 g/8 oz okra, trimmed and cut into 1 cm/½ in slices
30 ml/2 tbsp chopped fresh coriander
basmati rice, to serve

FOR THE MANGO RELISH
1 large ripe mango, about 500 g/1¼ lb in weight
1 small garlic clove, crushed
1 onion, finely chopped
10 ml/2 tsp grated fresh ginger root
1 fresh red chilli, seeded and finely chopped
pinch of salt and sugar

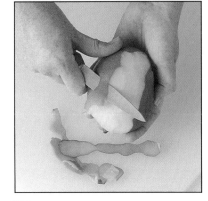

onion

ginger

garlic

cumin seeds

mango

mushrooms

okra

red chillies

chopped tomatoes

coriander seeds

turmeric

cardamom pods

 For the mango relish, peel the mango and cut off the flesh from the stone.

2 In a bowl mash the mango flesh with a fork or pulse in a food processor, and mix in the rest of the relish ingredients. Set to one side.

3 Place the garlic, ginger, chilli and 45 ml/3 tbsp of the water into a blender and blend until smooth.

4 Heat the sunflower oil in a large pan. Add the whole coriander and cumin seeds and allow them to sizzle for a few seconds. Add the ground cumin, ground cardamom and turmeric and cook for 1 minute more.

NUTRITIONAL NOTES

Per portion:

ENERGY 141Kcals/595KJ PROTEIN 5.81g
FAT 5.18g SATURATED FAT 0.74g
CARBOHYDRATE 19.19g
FIBRE 6.77g SUGAR 17.23g
SODIUM 51.75mg

5 Add the paste from the blender, the tomatoes, remaining water, mushrooms and okra. Stir to mix well and bring to the boil. Reduce the heat, cover, and simmer for 5 minutes.

6 Remove the cover, turn up the heat slightly and cook for another 5–10 minutes until the okra is tender. Stir in the fresh coriander and serve with rice and the mango relish.

Ratatouille Penne Bake

Serves 6

INGREDIENTS

1 small aubergine, cubed
2 courgettes, sliced
200 g/7 oz firm tofu, cubed
30 ml/2 tbsp dark soy sauce
3 garlic cloves, crushed
10 ml/2 tsp sesame seeds
30 ml/2 tbsp olive oil
1 small red pepper, seeded and
    sliced
1 onion, finely chopped
150 ml/¼ pint/⅔ cup vegetable
stock
3 firm ripe tomatoes, skinned,
    seeded and quartered
15 ml/1 tbsp chopped mixed herbs
225 g/ 8 oz penne
salt and ground black pepper
crusty bread, to serve

1 Place the aubergine and courgettes in a colander. Sprinkle with salt and leave to drain for 30 minutes, then rinse well and pat dry.

2 Mix the tofu with the soy sauce, one of the garlic cloves and sesame seeds. Cover and marinate for 30 minutes. Meanwhile, sauté the aubergine and courgettes in the olive oil until lightly browned.

3 Put the pepper, onion and remaining garlic into a saucepan with the stock. Bring to the boil, cover and cook for 5 minutes until tender. Remove the lid and boil until all the stock has evaporated. Add the tomatoes and herbs and cook for a further 3 minutes. Season to taste.

4 Meanwhile cook the pasta in a large pan of boiling, salted water until *al dente*. Drain thoroughly. Toss the pasta with all the vegetables and tofu. Transfer to a shallow 25 cm/10 in square ovenproof dish and grill until lightly toasted. Transfer to a serving dish and serve with fresh crusty bread.

tomatoes

courgettes

aubergine

red pepper

tofu

garlic

onion   *penne*

sesame seeds

vegetable stock   *soy sauce*

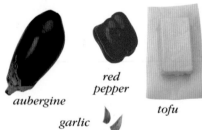

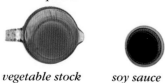

NUTRITIONAL NOTES
PER PORTION:

ENERGY 234Kcals/986KJ PROTEIN 9.03g
FAT 8.4g SATURATED FAT 1.19g
CARBOHYDRATE 32.6g
FIBRE 2.6g SUGAR 5.3g
SODIUM 364mg

Chilli Bean Bake

The contrasting textures of saucy beans, vegetables and crunchy cornbread topping make this a memorable meal.

Serves 4

INGREDIENTS
225 g/8 oz/1⅓ cups red kidney beans
1 bay leaf
1 large onion, finely chopped
1 garlic clove, crushed
2 celery sticks, sliced
5 ml/1 tsp ground cumin
5 ml/1 tsp chilli powder
400 g/14 oz can chopped tomatoes
15 ml/1 tbsp tomato purée
5 ml/1 tsp dried mixed herbs
15 ml/1 tbsp lemon juice
1 yellow pepper, seeded and diced
salt and freshly ground black pepper
mixed salad, to serve

FOR THE CORNBREAD TOPPING
175 g/6 oz/1½ cups corn meal
15 ml/1 tbsp wholemeal flour
5 ml/1 tsp baking powder
1 egg, beaten
175 ml/6 fl oz/¾ cup skimmed milk

kidney beans

celery

tomato purée

pepper

NUTRITIONAL NOTES
PER PORTION:

ENERGY 396.75Kcals/1676KJ PROTEIN 22.73g
FAT 4.67g SATURATED FAT 0.65g
CARBOHYDRATE 68.75g
FIBRE 11.9g SUGAR 9.89g
SODIUM 272mg

1 Soak the beans overnight in cold water. Drain and rinse well. Pour 1 litre/1¾ pints/4 cups of water into a large, heavy-based saucepan together with the beans and bay leaf and boil rapidly for 10 minutes. Lower the heat, cover and simmer for 35–40 minutes, or until the beans are tender.

2 Add the onion, garlic clove, celery, cumin, chilli powder, chopped tomatoes, tomato purée and dried mixed herbs. Half-cover the pan with a lid and simmer for a further 10 minutes.

3 Stir in the lemon juice, yellow pepper and seasoning. Simmer for a further 8-10 minutes, stirring occasionally, until the vegetables are just tender. Discard the bay leaf and spoon the mixture into a large casserole.

4 Pre-heat the oven to 220°C/425°F/Gas 7. For the topping, put the corn meal, flour, baking powder and a pinch of salt into a bowl and mix together. Make a well in the centre and add the egg and milk. Mix and pour over the bean mixture. Bake in the pre-heated oven for 20 minutes, or until brown.

Vegetable Biryani

This exotic dish made from everyday ingredients will be appreciated by vegetarians and meat eaters alike.

Serves 4–6

NUTRITIONAL NOTES
PER PORTION:

ENERGY 152Kcals/644KJ PROTEIN 4.5g
FAT 1.18g SATURATED FAT 0.1g
CARBOHYDRATE 34.16g
FIBRE 1.86g SUGAR 3.22g
SODIUM 0.05mg

INGREDIENTS
175 g/6 oz/1 cup long-grain rice
2 whole cloves
seeds of 2 cardamom pods
450 ml/¾ pint/scant 2 cups
  vegetable stock
2 garlic cloves
1 small onion, roughly chopped
5 ml/1 tsp cumin seeds
5 ml/1 tsp ground coriander
2.5 ml/½ tsp ground turmeric
2.5 ml/½ tsp chilli powder
1 large potato, peeled and cut into
  2.5 cm/1 in cubes
2 carrots, sliced
½ cauliflower, broken into florets
50 g/2 oz French beans, cut into
  2.5 cm/1 in lengths
30 ml/2 tbsp chopped fresh coriander
30 ml/2 tbsp lime juice
salt and freshly ground black pepper
sprig of fresh coriander, to garnish

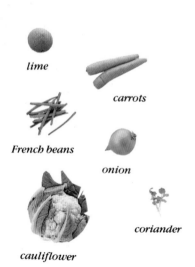

lime

carrots

French beans

onion

coriander

cauliflower

1 Put the rice, cloves and cardamom seeds into a large, heavy-based saucepan. Pour over the stock and bring to the boil.

2 Reduce the heat, cover and simmer for 20 minutes, or until all the stock has been absorbed.

3 Meanwhile put the garlic cloves, onion, cumin seeds, coriander, turmeric, chilli powder and seasoning into a blender or coffee grinder together with 30 ml/ 2 tbsp water. Blend to a paste.

4 Preheat the oven to 180°C/350°F/ Gas 4. Spoon the spicy paste into a flameproof casserole and cook over a low heat for 2 minutes, stirring occasionally.

5 Add the potato, carrots, cauliflower, beans and 90 ml/6 tbsp water. Cover and cook over a low heat for a further 12 minutes, stirring occasionally. Add the chopped coriander.

6 Spoon the rice over the vegetables. Sprinkle over the lime juice. Cover and cook in the oven for 25 minutes, or until the vegetables are tender. Fluff up the rice with a fork before serving and garnish with a sprig of fresh coriander.

Spinach and Potato Galette

Creamy layers of potato, spinach and herbs make a warming supper dish.

Serves 6

INGREDIENTS
900 g/2 lb large potatoes
450 g/1 lb fresh spinach
2 eggs
400 g/14 oz/1¾ cup low-fat cream
  cheese
15 ml/1 tbsp grainy mustard
50 g/2 oz chopped fresh herbs
  (e.g. chives, parsley, chervil or
  sorrel)
salt and freshly ground black pepper

mustard
parsley
cream cheese
spinach
egg
potatoes
chives
cherry tomatoes
chervil
sorrel

NUTRITIONAL NOTES
PER PORTION:

ENERGY 230.83Kcals/972.16KJ PROTEIN 17.27g
FAT 5.98g SATURATED FAT 0.65g
CARBOHYDRATE 28.57g
FIBRE 3.77g SUGAR 3.58g
SODIUM 438.66mg

1 Preheat the oven to 180°C/350°F/ Gas 4. Line a deep 23 cm/9 in cake tin with non-stick baking paper. Place the potatoes in a large pan and cover with cold water. Bring to the boil and cook for 10 minutes. Drain well and allow to cool slightly before slicing thinly.

2 Wash the spinach and place in a large pan with only the water that is clinging to the leaves. Cover and cook, stirring once, until the spinach has just wilted. Drain well in a sieve and squeeze out the excess moisture. Chop finely.

3 Beat the eggs with the cream cheese and mustard then stir in the chopped spinach and fresh herbs.

4 Place a layer of the sliced potatoes in the lined tin, arranging them in concentric circles. Top with a spoonful of the cream cheese mixture and spread out. Continue layering, seasoning with salt and pepper as you go, until all the potatoes and the cream cheese mixture are used up.

5 Cover the tin with a piece of foil and place in a roasting tin.

6 Fill the roasting tin with enough boiling water to come halfway up the sides, and cook in the oven for 45–50 minutes. Turn out onto a plate and serve hot or cold.

Mixed Mushroom Ragout

These mushrooms are delicious served hot or cold and can be made up to two days in advance.

Serves 4

1 small onion, finely chopped
1 garlic clove, crushed
5 ml/1 tsp coriander seeds, crushed
30 ml/2 tbsp red wine vinegar
15 ml/1 tbsp soy sauce
15 ml/1 tbsp dry sherry
10 ml/2 tsp tomato purée
10 ml/2 tsp soft light brown sugar
150 ml/¼ pint/⅔ cup vegetable stock
115 g/4 oz baby button mushrooms
115 g/4 oz chestnut mushrooms, quartered
115 g/4 oz oyster mushrooms, sliced
salt and freshly ground black pepper
sprig of fresh coriander, to garnish

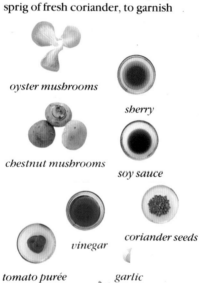

oyster mushrooms

sherry

chestnut mushrooms

soy sauce

vinegar

coriander seeds

tomato purée

garlic

coriander

button mushrooms

onion

NUTRITIONAL NOTES
Per portion:

ENERGY 36Kcals/152KJ PROTEIN 2.25g
FAT 0.63g SATURATED FAT 0.07g
CARBOHYDRATE 4.92g
FIBRE 0.94g SUGAR 4.04g
SODIUM 32.75mg

1 Put the first nine ingredients into a large saucepan. Bring to the boil and reduce the heat. Cover and simmer for 5 minutes.

2 Uncover the saucepan and simmer for 5 more minutes, or until the liquid has reduced by half.

3 Add the baby button and chestnut mushrooms and simmer for 3 minutes. Stir in the oyster mushrooms and cook for a further 2 minutes.

4 Remove the mushrooms with a slotted spoon and transfer them to a serving dish.

5 Boil the juices for about 5 minutes, or until reduced to about 75 ml/5 tbsp. Season to taste.

6 Allow to cool for 2-3 minutes, then pour over the mushrooms. Serve hot or well chilled, garnished with a sprig of fresh coriander.

Lemon Hearts with Strawberry Sauce

These elegant little hearts are light as air, and they are best made the day before your dinner party – which saves on last-minute panics as well!

Serves 6

INGREDIENTS
FOR THE HEARTS
175 g/6 oz/¾ cup ricotta cheese
150 ml/¼ pint/⅔ cup crème fraîche
   or soured cream
15 ml/1 tbsp granulated sweetener
finely grated rind of ½ lemon
30 ml/2 tbsp lemon juice
10 ml/2 tsp powdered gelatine
2 egg whites

FOR THE SAUCE
225 g/8 oz/2 cups fresh or frozen and
   thawed strawberries
15 ml/1 tbsp lemon juice

ricotta cheese

crème fraîche

powdered gelatine

lemon

strawberries

eggs

granulated sweetener

1 Beat the ricotta cheese until smooth. Stir in the crème fraîche, sweetener and lemon rind.

2 Place the lemon juice in a small bowl and sprinkle the gelatine over it. Place the bowl over a pan of hot water and stir to dissolve the gelatine completely.

3 Quickly stir the gelatine into the cheese mixture, mixing it in evenly.

4 Beat the egg whites until they form soft peaks. Quickly fold them into the cheese mixture.

5 Spoon the mixture into six lightly oiled, individual heart-shaped moulds and chill the moulds until set.

VARIATION

These little heart-shaped desserts are the perfect choice for a romantic dinner, but they don't have to be heart-shaped – try setting the mixture in individual fluted moulds, or even in ordinary teacups.

NUTRITIONAL NOTES

PER PORTION:

ENERGY 113.33Kcals/470.8KJ PROTEIN 6.15g
FAT 8.22g SATURATED FAT 5.14g
CARBOHYDRATE 3.9g
FIBRE 0.42g SUGAR 3.9g
SODIUM 67.5mg

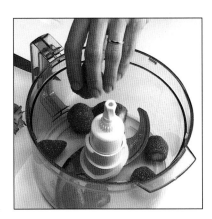

6 Place the strawberries and lemon juice in a blender and process until smooth. Pour the sauce on to serving plates and place the turned-out hearts on top. Decorate with slices of strawberry.

Minted Raspberry Bavarois

A sophisticated dessert that can be made a day in advance for a special dinner party.

Serves 6

INGREDIENTS
450 g/1 lb/5½ cups fresh or frozen
   and thawed raspberries
30 ml/2 tbsp icing sugar
30 ml/2 tbsp lemon juice
15 ml/1 tbsp finely chopped fresh mint
30 ml/2 tbsp/2 sachets powdered
   gelatine
75 ml/5 tbsp boiling water
300 ml/½ pint/1¼ cups custard,
   made with skimmed milk
250 g/9 oz/1⅛ cups Greek yogurt
fresh mint sprigs, to decorate

skimmed-milk custard

icing sugar

Greek yogurt

powdered gelatine

lemon

mint

raspberries

1 Reserve a few raspberries for decoration. Place the raspberries, icing sugar and lemon juice in a food processor and process them until smooth.

2 Press the purée through a sieve to remove the raspberry pips. Add the mint. You should have about 500 ml/1 pint/2½ cups of purée.

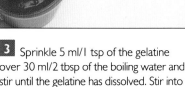

3 Sprinkle 5 ml/1 tsp of the gelatine over 30 ml/2 tbsp of the boiling water and stir until the gelatine has dissolved. Stir into 150 ml/¼ pint/⅔ cup of the fruit purée.

4 Pour this jelly into a 1-litre/1¾-pint/4-cup mould, and leave the mould to chill in the refrigerator until the jelly is just on the point of setting. Tip the tin to swirl the setting jelly around the sides, and then leave to chill until the jelly has set completely.

5 Stir the remaining fruit purée into the custard and yogurt. Dissolve the rest of the gelatine in the remaining water and stir it in quickly.

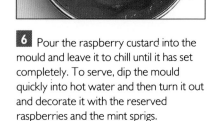

6 Pour the raspberry custard into the mould and leave it to chill until it has set completely. To serve, dip the mould quickly into hot water and then turn it out and decorate it with the reserved raspberries and the mint sprigs.

NUTRITIONAL NOTES
PER PORTION:

ENERGY 144.16Kcals/611.66KJ PROTEIN 9.95g
FAT 4.08g SATURATED FAT 2.29g
CARBOHYDRATE 18.13g
FIBRE 1.88g SUGAR 15.35g
SODIUM 89.83mg

Grilled Nectarines with Ricotta and Spice

This easy dessert is good at any time of year – use canned peach halves if fresh ones are not available.

Serves 4

INGREDIENTS
4 ripe nectarines or peaches
15 ml/1 tbsp light muscovado sugar
115 g/4 oz/½ cup ricotta cheese or
    fromage frais
2.5 ml/½ tsp ground star anise

nectarines

light muscovado sugar

ricotta cheese

ground star anise

NUTRITIONAL NOTES
PER PORTION:

ENERGY 136.25Kcals/577.25KJ PROTEIN 5.52g
FAT 3.36g SATURATED FAT 1.98g
CARBOHYDRATE 22.49g
FIBRE 2.4g SUGAR 22.49g
SODIUM 31mg

COOK'S TIP
Star anise has a warm, rich flavour – if you can't get it, try ground cloves or ground mixed spice instead.

1 Cut the nectarines in half and remove the stones.

2 Arrange the nectarines, cut-side upwards, in a wide flameproof dish or on a baking sheet.

3 Stir the sugar into the ricotta or fromage frais. Using a teaspoon, spoon the mixture into the hollow of each nectarine half.

4 Sprinkle with the star anise. Place under a moderately hot grill for 6–8 minutes, or until the nectarines are hot and bubbling. Serve warm.

Golden Ginger Compote

Warm, spicy and full of sun-ripened ingredients – this is the perfect winter dessert.

Serves 4

INGREDIENTS
200 g/7 oz/2 cups kumquats
200 g/7 oz/1¼ cups dried apricots
30 ml/2 tbsp sultanas
400 ml/14 fl oz/1⅔ cups water
1 orange
2.5 cm/1 in piece fresh root ginger
4 cardamom pods
4 cloves
30 ml/2 tbsp clear honey
15 ml/1 tbsp flaked almonds, toasted

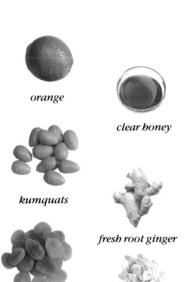

orange

clear honey

kumquats

fresh root ginger

dried apricots

flaked almonds

cloves

cardamom pods

sultanas

1 Wash the kumquats, and, if they are large, cut them in half. Place them in a pan with the apricots, sultanas and water. Bring to the boil.

2 Pare the rind thinly from the orange and add to the pan. Peel and grate the ginger; lightly crush the cardamom pods and add to the pan with the cloves.

NUTRITIONAL NOTES

PER PORTION:

ENERGY 196.75Kcals/836KJ PROTEIN 4.57g
FAT 3.11g SATURATED FAT 0.23g
CARBOHYDRATE 41.18g
FIBRE 6.85g SUGAR 40.92g
SODIUM 39.25mg

3 Reduce the heat, cover the pan and leave to simmer gently for about 30 minutes, or until the fruit is tender, stirring occasionally.

4 Squeeze the juice from the orange and add to the pan with honey to sweeten to taste, sprinkle with flaked almonds and serve warm.

Fresh Citrus Jelly

Fresh fruit jellies really are worth the effort – they're packed with fresh flavour, natural colour and vitamins – and they make a lovely fat-free dessert.

Serves 4

INGREDIENTS
3 medium-size oranges
1 lemon
1 lime
300 ml/½ pint/1¼ cups water
75 g/3 oz/⅓ cup golden caster sugar
15 ml/1 tbsp/1 sachet powdered
  gelatine
extra slices of fruit, to decorate

powdered gelatine

golden caster sugar

lime

oranges

lemon

1 With a sharp knife, cut all the peel and white pith from one orange and carefully remove the segments. Arrange the segments in the base of a 900 ml/1½-pint/3¾-cup mould or dish.

2 Remove some shreds of citrus rind with a zester and reserve them for decoration. Grate the remaining rind from the lemon and lime and one orange. Place all the grated rind in a pan, with the water and sugar.

3 Heat gently until the sugar has dissolved, without boiling. Remove from the heat. Squeeze the juice from all the rest of the fruit and stir it into the pan.

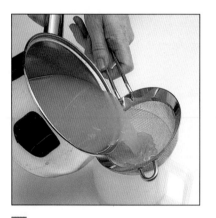

4 Strain the liquid into a measuring jug to remove the rind (you should have about 550 ml/1 pint/2½ cups: if necessary, make up the amount with water). Sprinkle the gelatine over the liquid and stir until it has completely dissolved.

5 Pour a little of the jelly over the orange segments and chill until set. Leave the remaining jelly at room temperature to cool, but do not allow it to set.

COOK'S TIP

To speed up the setting of the fruit segments in jelly, stand the dish in a bowl of ice. Or, if you're short of time, simply stir the segments into the liquid jelly, pour into a serving dish and set it all together.

NUTRITIONAL NOTES

PER PORTION:

ENERGY 132.25Kcals/563.75KJ PROTEIN 4.56g
FAT 0.15g SATURATED FAT 0.01g
CARBOHYDRATE 30g
FIBRE 2.04g SUGAR 30g
SODIUM 19.75mg

6 Pour the remaining cooled jelly into the dish and chill until set. To serve, turn out the jelly and decorate it with the reserved citrus rind shreds and slices of citrus fruit.

Poached Pears in Maple-yogurt Sauce

An elegant dessert that is easier to make than it looks – poach the pears in advance, and have the cooled syrup ready to spoon on to the plates just before you serve.

Serves 6

INGREDIENTS
6 firm dessert pears
15 ml/1 tbsp lemon juice
250 ml/8 fl oz/1 cup sweet white wine
   or cider
thinly pared rind of 1 lemon
1 cinnamon stick
30 ml/2 tbsp maple syrup
2.5 ml/½ tsp arrowroot
150 g/5 oz/⅔ cup Greek yogurt

sweet white wine

Greek yogurt

pears

maple syrup

lemon

arrowroot

cinnamon stick

NUTRITIONAL NOTES
PER PORTION:

ENERGY 134Kcals/563KJ PROTEIN 2.16g
FAT 2.44g SATURATED FAT 1.3g
CARBOHYDRATE 20.54g
FIBRE 3.52g SUGAR 19.83g
SODIUM 28.5mg

COOK'S TIP

The cooking time will vary, depending upon the type and ripeness of the pears. The pears should be ripe, but still firm – over-ripe ones will not keep their shape well.

1 Thinly peel the pears, leaving them whole and with stalks. Brush them with lemon juice, to prevent them from browning. Use a potato peeler or small knife to scoop out the core from the base of each pear.

2 Place the pears in a wide, heavy pan and pour over the wine, with enough cold water almost to cover the pears.

3 Add the lemon rind and cinnamon stick, and then bring to the boil. Reduce the heat, cover the pan and simmer the pears gently for 30–40 minutes, or until tender. Turn the pears occasionally so that they cook evenly. Lift out the pears carefully, draining them well.

4 Bring the liquid to the boil and boil uncovered to reduce to about 100 ml/ 4 fl oz/½ cup. Strain and add the maple syrup. Blend a little of the liquid with the arrowroot. Return to the pan and cook, stirring, until thick and clear. Cool.

5 Slice each pear about three-quarters of the way through, leaving the slices attached at the stem end. Fan each pear out on a serving plate.

6 Stir 30 ml/2 tbsp of the cooled syrup into the yogurt and spoon it around the pears. Drizzle with the remaining syrup and serve immediately.

Frozen Apple and Blackberry Terrine

Apples and blackberries are a classic autumn combination; they really complement each other. This pretty, three-layered terrine can be frozen, so you can enjoy it at any time of year.

Serves 6

INGREDIENTS

500 g/1 lb cooking or eating apples
300 ml/½ pint/1¼ cups sweet cider
15 ml/1 tbsp clear honey
5 ml/1 tsp vanilla essence
200 g/7 oz/2 cups fresh or frozen and thawed blackberries
15 ml/1 tbsp/1 sachet powdered gelatine
2 egg whites
fresh apple slices and blackberries, to decorate

sweet cider

vanilla essence

clear honey

eggs

blackberries

powdered gelatine

VARIATION

For a quicker version the mixture can be set without the layering. Purée the apples and blackberries together, stir the dissolved gelatine and whisked egg whites into the mixture, turn the whole thing into the tin and leave the mixture to set.

1 Peel, core and chop the apples and place them in a pan, with half the cider. Bring the cider to the boil, and then cover the pan and let the apples simmer gently until tender.

2 Tip the apples into a food processor and process them to a smooth purée. Stir in the honey and vanilla. Add half the blackberries to half the apple purée, and then process again until smooth. Sieve to remove the pips.

3 Heat the remaining cider until it's almost boiling, and then sprinkle the gelatine over and stir until the gelatine has completely dissolved. Add half the gelatine to the apple purée and half to the blackberry purée.

4 Leave the purées to cool until almost set. Whisk the egg whites until they are stiff. Quickly fold them into the apple purée. Remove half the purée to another bowl. Stir the remaining whole blackberries into half the apple purée, and then tip this into a 1.75-litre/3-pint/7½-cup loaf tin, packing it down firmly.

5 Top with the blackberry purée and spread it evenly. Finally, add a layer of the apple purée and smooth it evenly. If necessary, freeze each layer until firm before adding the next.

6 Freeze until firm. To serve, allow to stand at room temperature for about 20 minutes to soften, and then serve in slices, decorated with fresh apples and blackberries.

Passion-fruit and Apple Foam

Passion-fruit have an exotic, scented flavour that makes this simple apple dessert very special; if passion-fruit are not available, use two finely chopped kiwi fruit instead.

Serves 4

INGREDIENTS
500 g/1 lb cooking apples
90 ml/6 tbsp apple juice
3 passion-fruit
3 egg whites
1 red-skinned apple, to decorate
lemon juice

apple juice

lemon

cooking apples

red-skinned apple

eggs

passion-fruit

NUTRITIONAL NOTES
Per portion:
ENERGY 74Kcals/318KJ PROTEIN 2.93g
FAT 0.21g SATURATED FAT 0.012g
CARBOHYDRATE 16.27g
FIBRE 2.75g SUGAR 16.27g
SODIUM 51.25mg

1 Peel, core and roughly chop the cooking apples and place them in a pan, with the apple juice.

2 Bring to the boil, and then reduce the heat and cover the pan. Cook gently, stirring occasionally, until the apple is very tender.

3 Remove from the heat and beat the apple mixture with a wooden spoon until it becomes a fairly smooth purée (or purée the apple in a food processor).

4 Cut the passion-fruit in half and scoop out the flesh. Stir the flesh into the apple purée.

5 Place the egg whites in a clean, dry bowl and whisk them until they form soft peaks. Fold the egg whites into the apple mixture. Spoon the apple foam into four serving dishes.

COOK'S TIP

It's important to use a good cooking apple, such as a Bramley, for this recipe, because the fluffy texture of a cooking apple breaks down easily to a purée. You can use dessert apples, but you will find it easier to purée them in a food processor.

6 Thinly slice the red-skinned apple and brush the slices with lemon juice, to prevent them from browning. Arrange the slices on top of the apple foam and serve cold.

Strawberry and Apple Crumble

A high-fibre, healthier version of the classic apple crumble.

Serves 4

INGREDIENTS

450 g/1 lb cooking apples
150 g/5 oz/1¼ cups strawberries
30 ml/2 tbsp granulated sweetener
2.5 ml/½ tsp ground cinnamon
30 ml/2 tbsp orange juice

FOR THE CRUMBLE
45 ml/3 tbsp plain wholemeal flour
50 g/2 oz/⅔ cup porridge oats
25g/1 oz/⅛ cup low-fat spread

NUTRITIONAL NOTES
PER PORTION:

ENERGY 161.5Kcals/684.5KJ PROTEIN 4.02g
FAT 4.02g SATURATED FAT 0.73g
CARBOHYDRATE 29.24g
FIBRE 4.08g SUGAR 13.19g
SODIUM 50.25mg

porridge oats

granulated sweetener

low-fat spread

wholemeal flour

strawberries

cooking apples

ground cinnamon

1 Preheat the oven to 180°C/350°F/Gas 4. Peel, core and slice the apples. Hull and halve the strawberries.

2 Toss together the apples, strawberries, sweetener, cinnamon and orange juice. Tip into a 1.2-litre/2-pint/5-cup ovenproof dish, or four individual dishes.

3 Combine the flour and oats in a bowl and mix in the low-fat spread with a fork.

4 Sprinkle the crumble evenly over the fruit. Bake for 40–45 minutes (20–25 minutes for individual dishes), until golden brown and bubbling. Serve warm, with custard or yogurt.

Angel Cake

Serve this light-as-air cake with low fat fromage frais – it makes a perfect dessert.

Serves 10

INGREDIENTS

40 g/1½ oz/⅓ cup cornflour
40 g/1½ oz/⅓ cup plain flour
8 egg whites
225 g/8 oz/1 cup caster sugar, plus
  extra for sprinkling
5 ml/1 tsp vanilla essence
icing sugar, for dusting

cornflour

vanilla essence

plain flour

caster sugar

eggs

NUTRITIONAL NOTES

PER PORTION:

ENERGY 125.7Kcals/535.5KJ PROTEIN 2.7g
FAT 0.08g SATURATED FAT 0.01g
CARBOHYDRATE 30.4g
FIBRE 0.128g SUGAR 23.68g
SODIUM 52mg

1 Preheat the oven to 180°C/350°F/Gas 4. Sift both flours on to a sheet of greaseproof paper.

2 Whisk the egg whites in a large grease-free bowl until very stiff, then gradually add the sugar and vanilla essence, whisking until the mixture is thick and glossy.

COOK'S TIP

Make a lemony icing by mixing 175 g/6 oz/1½ cups icing sugar with 15–30 ml/1–2 tbsp lemon juice. Drizzle the icing over the cake and decorate with physalis or lemon slices and mint sprigs.

3 Gently fold in the flour mixture with a large metal spoon. Spoon into an ungreased 25 cm/10 in angel cake tin, smooth the surface and bake for about 45–50 minutes, until the cake springs back when lightly pressed.

4 Sprinkle a piece of greaseproof paper with caster sugar and set an egg cup in the centre. Invert the cake tin over the paper, balancing it carefully on the egg cup. When cold, the cake will drop out of the tin. Transfer it to a plate, decorate if liked (see Cook's Tip), then dust with icing sugar and serve.

INDEX